THE NE\

The Supe

CW00621284

PREGNANCY
GUIDE
FOR MEN

Master the Nine-Month Journey and Become the Ultimate Supportive
Partner by Unlocking Secret Tips & Hacks for First-Time Fathers
(Handbook for Dads-to-Be)

MADDOX & FLORA KING

Get Your Free Bonuses Now!

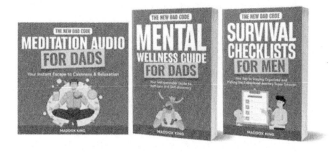

BONUS # 1: Survival Checklists for Dads

Your Key to Staying Organized and Making the Pregnancy Journey Super Smooth!

BONUS # 2: Mental Wellness Guide for Dads

Your Indispensable Guide to Self-care and Self-discovery, Ensuring a Journey Towards a Happier and More Fulfilled You!

BONUS # 3: Meditation Audio for Dads

Your Instant Escape to Calmness, Relaxation, and Well-deserved Quality "Me Time."

Scan with your phone's camera **OR** go to: https://bit.ly/47YIMsV

CONTENTS

INTRODUCTION

I'm standing in the middle of a bustling IKEA, staring at a crib's assembly instructions that might as well be hieroglyphics. On my left, a young couple is debating the merits of organic versus non-organic baby wipes. To my right, a pregnant woman, who could go into labor at any minute, is instructing her partner on the importance of getting the perfect shade of blue for the nursery. And there I am, amidst it all, wondering, "Is there a course on how to be a dad, and why didn't I enroll in it?"

If you're reading this, chances are, you can relate to the excitement, apprehension, and whirlwind of emotions that come with the knowledge that you're about to be responsible for another human life. But with the joy also comes the pressure—from picking the right baby gear and understanding what's happening with your partner's body to grappling with the financial, emotional, and lifestyle changes that a baby brings.

You might be thinking, "Why is pregnancy so complicated for fathers?" As men, we aren't just bystanders. We're active participants in this journey, albeit without the morning sickness and swollen ankles. Yet, while our partners have an array of pregnancy books, apps, and mommy blogs, we're often left wondering where our manual is. Where's the guide that breaks down the dad's role in pregnancy, labor, and those life-altering first months of parenthood?

That's where this book comes in. I'm Maddox King, a born-and-raised Californian in his mid-40s, juggling the roles of seasoned software engineer and dad to three amazing kids (not to mention our two mischievous dogs). Yeah, life's a riot in the King household!

You'd think being an engineer—someone who thrives on solving puzzles—would have given me an edge when it came time to step into the realm of crying babies, midnight feedings, and lots of diapers. I approached fatherhood with the same rigor I applied to my projects—diving deep, researching, and engaging in a fair amount of trial and error. Natalie, my firstborn, was the start of a crazy adventure full of those, "Well, I didn't see that coming!" moments.

Even with all of my analytical prowess and "engineer's mindset," there were moments when I felt entirely out of my depth. I quickly learned that, sometimes, the best solution isn't fixing a problem, but just being there, supportive and present. For me, this journey was filled with laughter, frustration, 3:00 AM dances to soothe crying babies, and the inexplicable joy of watching my children take their first steps.

With three kids in tow, I've had my fair share of parenting epiphanies. And trust me, each one was an adventure unto itself—a puzzle that required a different approach. Over the years, I've honed my fathering skills, diving deep into the nuances of parenting—especially from the perspective of a dad. My five-year-long quest to understand the essence of fatherhood, coupled with my firsthand experiences, shaped my journey and gave birth to this guide.

This isn't just a technical manual penned by a detached author in an ivory tower. This is my heart and soul—and a generous sprinkle of those "Oops, I did it again" moments. This book is a testament to my belief that every dad, whether they are elbow-deep in code or not, can navigate the choppy waters of fatherhood with grace, humor, and a whole lot of love.

What sets this book apart? It's tailored for you—the modern man who's not just looking to be a provider, but who wants to be actively involved, emotionally connected, and the best possible partner. This is a book for the dad who wants to understand what's happening during each trimester—the man who seeks to know why his wife is craving pickles dipped in chocolate at 2:00 AM, and who's just trying to figure out how to assemble a crib without losing his sanity.

Remember those legendary tales we read as kids about explorers braving new worlds and venturing into the unknown? Think of this journey into fatherhood as your own personal expedition. You will encounter the wilderness of diaper changes, the treacherous terrain of sleepless nights, and the elation of reaching milestones like your child's first smile. Like any explorer, your biggest asset isn't the equipment you carry (though a sturdy diaper bag does help), but rather the attitude you possess. A sense of humor will be your compass, love will be your map, and patience will be your most trusty hiking boots.

I recall one of my earliest experiences, when I was trying to master the fine art of swaddling. It seemed simple enough, yet my daughter ended up looking more like a mini-burrito than the serene, swaddled baby on the package. And let's not even get into my first attempt at a diaper change. Suffice to say, it was...explosive. In moments like these, I realized that no amount of reading or preparation can truly prepare you for the unpredictable joys and challenges of fatherhood. But, that being said, having a guide sure makes the journey smoother.

In this book, we'll delve into the practical, emotional, and sometimes downright hilarious aspects of being an expectant father. We'll demystify those nine months leading up to delivery day, ensuring you're well-prepared—whether it's choosing the right car seat or knowing the secret tricks to soothe a crying baby. And, at the end of each chapter, we've added a special section: "From a Woman's Perspective." These are not general statements from random mothers, but heartfelt words directly from my own wife. She has graciously penned down her thoughts, emotions, and the tidbits she wished I was privy to during her pregnancies, providing an authentic and intimate peek into the maternal psyche.

"Why trust me?" you may ask. Beyond my own paternal escapades, I've interviewed countless dads, sourced wisdom from experienced parents, and even picked the brains of obstetricians and pediatricians. Every anecdote, strategy, and bit of advice in this book is rooted in real-life experiences, ensuring that the guidance is practical, profoundly personal, and backed up by real evidence.

Before we dive in, let me leave you with a thought. Parenthood is a roller coaster, complete with exhilarating highs and a few nerve-wracking drops. But remember, roller coasters are a heck of a lot of fun. So, strap in and get ready to enjoy the ride. Let's embark on this exciting journey of fatherhood together.

Chapter One

DECODING THE FIRST TRIMESTER: NAVIGATING EARLY PREGNANCY

"Every child begins the world anew, both for himself and for his parents."

— *Charles Dickens*

So, you just got the news. You're about to embark on a life-changing journey—one that's filled with more plot twists than a bestselling novel. The first trimester is like the initial chapters of this story, setting the tone for the incredible adventure ahead.

Even though I could swiftly decode complex software problems in my previous life, nothing quite prepared me for this intricate dance of biology, emotions, and late-night pickle runs.

Growing a Human: What's Happening to Baby and Mom

From the moment the pregnancy test shows those two distinct lines, both the baby and the mom undergo some monumental transformations. The baby is essentially being built from scratch, starting from a single cell and growing into a whole new person. Meanwhile, a mom's body is changing in amazing ways to make this happen.

Quick stats/description for Mom and Baby:

0-4w:

- **Mom:** Might still be oblivious to the fact that she's pregnant, but her body starts increasing the production of hormones like progesterone and human chorionic gonadotropin (hCG).
- **Baby:** About the size of a poppy seed. It's essentially a ball of cells right now, but it's rapidly dividing and developing.

5-8w:

- **Mom:** Morning sickness might come knocking. There's also an increase in fatigue, and she might be making frequent trips to the bathroom.
- **Baby:** Growing at a lightning pace! Developing tiny arm and leg buds. The heart begins to beat and organs start to form.

9-12w:

- **Mom:** Morning sickness may peak around this time. There's a glow on her face, but she's probably more interested in that cozy bed.
- **Baby:** Baby's fingers and toes are distinct now. All major organs are formed and start their preliminary functions. Baby might even start moving, although it's usually too early for Mom to feel.

As fascinating as these changes are, the ride isn't always smooth. It's a lot like my first experience as a software engineer. I remember when I encountered my first bug—a seemingly insurmountable glitch. The initial weeks of pregnancy can sometimes feel like that for the expectant mother—and, by extension, you! There's a mix of elation, bewilderment, and occasional bouts of nausea (and not just for her). But just like I dove deep into code, learning its nuances to solve that glitch, by diving deep into the first trimester, you'll be better prepared to support and understand your partner.

As we proceed, we'll be touching upon some of the immediate reactions after the "We're pregnant" news, and also how to ride the hormonal tidal wave. If you've ever felt like you're in over your head, wondering how on earth to be the anchor your partner needs—or simply curious about why she's suddenly repelled by the scent of your aftershave—don't fret. This chapter is your cheat code.

The Pregnancy Bombshell: Dealing with the "We're Pregnant" News

There's nothing quite like it—that pivotal moment when a regular evening transforms into a life-altering event. Your partner, a cascade of emotions flickering in her eyes, proclaims, "We're pregnant!" The universe simultaneously compresses and expands, enveloping you in a tidal wave of thoughts and feelings. Is this real? Am I prepared? What's the next step?

I've lived that moment—pausing a coding problem to be presented with the most delightful and bewildering puzzle of my life, symbolized by two little lines on a stick held by my teary-eyed, laughing partner. In that instant, my identity evolved from a debugger of code to a future debugger of baby-related mysteries.

Before we dive into what's ahead, let's enjoy this moment. It's big, exciting, and a little bit explosive.

While the emotional aspect is important, there's also a practical side to this bombshell that warrants attention. Here are a few initial steps you might consider taking after getting that positive test result:

1. **Confirmation from the OB:** While home pregnancy tests are pretty reliable, scheduling an appointment with an obstetrician (OB) for a professional confirmation is a prudent next step. This is where your partner will undergo a blood test for conclusive confirmation.

2. **Mind the False Positives:** False positives occasionally happen due to various factors, like certain medical conditions and medications. This is why an OB visit is so important. Note that a phenomenon known as a "chemical pregnancy"—a very early pregnancy loss—can also cause a positive test result, further underscoring the importance of professional confirmation.

3. **Dietary Adjustments:** This is an essential early move! Even though we will delve deeper into this in a later section, understanding that certain foods and beverages (like alcohol and high-mercury fish) should be avoided or minimized is crucial from the get-go.

4. **To Share or not to Share:** Deciding whether to immediately share the news or bask privately in its glow for a while is a personal choice. Some people prefer to wait until after the first trimester, when the risk of complications generally decreases.

When I first plunged into impending fatherhood, I learned that mixing feelings with practical steps is the best way to handle things. As you go back and forth between figuring out life and getting excited about being a parent, remember that every moment is a step in this special journey.

The Hormone Hurricane: Navigating Mood Swings (Yours and Hers)

Prepare yourself, because the hormone journey involves both of you. While it's well-known that expectant mothers experience mood swings due to hormonal changes, it might surprise you to learn that many fathers-to-be undergo similar emotional shifts. This is called Couvade Syndrome (often referred to as "sympathetic pregnancy").

Though not a medically recognized condition, Couvade Syndrome has been noted in various cultures for centuries. Men experiencing this syndrome may undergo symptoms like weight gain, nausea, insomnia, and even mood swings. While its exact cause is still debated, some suggest it might be tied to changes in male hormones. Research indicates that future fathers can see a drop in testosterone and a rise in a type of estrogen called estradiol. This alteration may be nature's method of gearing men toward a more nurturing role.

But before we delve further into the father's journey, it's crucial to understand what's happening with the mother. Hormonal changes during pregnancy are intense. There's a surge in progesterone and estrogen, which are both vital for maintaining the pregnancy and preparing the body for breastfeeding. These fluctuations can lead to heightened emotions, fatigue, and changes in appetite. Additionally, the physical changes, potential discomforts, and looming responsibility of motherhood all play into the emotional landscape.

For mothers, there's not merely the joy of impending motherhood—there's also the need to cope with body changes, potential health concerns, and external pressures. As a partner, recognizing this can help you be more supportive. Lend a listening ear, practice patience, and offer comfort when she's feeling overwhelmed.

Now, back to the fathers. I recall a time when a diaper commercial brought tears to my eyes. Strange as it was, it demonstrated that we, as future dads, undergo a profound internal transformation. While popular culture might spotlight Mom's sudden food cravings or distaste for certain scents, don't forget that you're undergoing changes, too. Both your body and mind are preparing for the monumental role of fatherhood.

Pregnancy is a shared experience, filled with hormonal shifts and emotions for both parties. Communication is crucial during this time. Stay open and supportive, and understand that these nine months mark the beginning of a remarkable shared journey into parenthood.

Supporting Mom's Physical and Emotional Well-Being

While your concerns might center around baby gadgets or the dwindling state of your bank account, your partner is undergoing deep physical and emotional transformations. I recall a buddy mentioning during a casual hangout, "Man, my wife teared up because we ran out of cereal. Seriously, cereal!" Such moments, while seemingly small on the surface, offer insight into the profound changes she's grappling with.

Your partner is experiencing intense emotions, all while nurturing a growing life inside her. Hormonal shifts can amplify feelings, leading to mood swings—from pure elation to sudden sadness. Physically, she's dealing with symptoms like nausea and fatigue, coupled with the wonder and occasional discomfort of a changing body.

Your role in all of this is multifaceted.

First, educate yourself about the pregnancy journey. Understand the changes she's experiencing during each trimester. Having this knowledge equips you to anticipate her needs and fosters empathy.

Be patient and compassionate. Offer massages when her back aches, cook her favorite meal when she's exhausted, or simply be there so she has someone to vent to. Listen attentively when she wants to talk about the latest unexpected symptom or her anxieties about motherhood. Attend prenatal classes together, making it a team effort. And during those sleep-interrupting leg cramps at 3:00 AM, be the one to massage them away, holding her hand and reassuring her through the discomfort.

Your partner's pregnancy is both an individual experience and a shared journey for her, so step up, be informed, and provide the unwavering support she needs.

Morning Sickness Mania: Tackling Nausea with Love and Saltine Crackers

Allow me to share a tale of good intentions and an unexpected twist involving my friend, Jason. He thought, "What's more romantic than surprising my pregnant wife with her favorite lunch, made from scratch?" The smell of scrambled eggs, perfectly toasted bread, and freshly squeezed orange juice wafted through the air. Unfortunately, he didn't get the positive response he was looking for. Instead, she dashed to the bathroom, vomited, and then asked for something else to eat.

Jason found himself grappling with "morning sickness" in the middle of the afternoon, and realized that the term can be misleading. Contrary to what the name suggests, nausea during pregnancy isn't confined to the morning hours. A study published in BJOG: An International Journal of Obstetrics and Gynaecology found that the majority of pregnant women who experience nausea (about 80%) do so at various times throughout the day, not just in the morning. This study, which involved 256 women with either nausea alone or both nausea and vomiting, found that only a small fraction (1.8%) reported symptoms exclusively in the morning.

But don't despair! You have tools at your disposal. Jason soon discovered the wonder that is Saltine crackers—a humble, yet often effective remedy for soothing a queasy stomach. Keeping them handy (especially by the bed for a pre-get-up snack) can often prevent a rush to the restroom.

Your partner's palate and stomach are on a whimsical journey, dictated by hormonal changes and the tiny being blossoming within. Sometimes, that lovingly prepared meal might hit the spot—and sometimes it might trigger a dash to the toilet. Flexibility, understanding, and a hand ready with a comforting rub (or a bucket) are key.

Keep in mind that this isn't solely about physical changes and unexpected visits to the bathroom. Pregnancy intertwines physical and emotional factors, creating a tapestry that's sometimes beautiful and sometimes a bit tangled. Hormonal changes, like elevated levels of hCG, are rapidly occurring, potentially playing a role in her nausea and certainly playing with her emotions. Your role? Offer understanding, a listening ear, and an endless supply of Saltine crackers.

Pro Tip: While Saltine crackers can be a staple for many who are combatting nausea, they might not be enough for everyone. If your partner is still struggling with queasiness, consider trying ginger in various forms, like ginger candy or ginger tea. Ginger has long been touted for its nausea-relieving properties. Other common remedies include peppermint tea, vitamin B6 supplements, and acupressure wristbands. It might take some experimenting to find what works best for her, but your proactive approach and support can make all the difference.

With each page you turn in this book, you're not only acquiring knowledge, but also paving the way toward a smoother journey through pregnancy with your partner. Your support and understanding are fundamental during this time. Those minor acts of love (even fetching a bucket at 3:00 AM) do more than assist her—they build a stronger bond between you both. This strengthened connection creates a robust foundation for your growing family.

Doctor Visits and Ultrasound Excitement: Sharing the Journey Together & What to Expect

Walking into that first prenatal doctor's visit with my wife, I felt like a fish flopping on the dock, gawking at the new world around me. The waiting room bustled with expectant mothers and partners, all various shades of excitement, with anxiety painted across their faces, mirroring my own internal tumult. In that moment, I realized that OB visits were a foreign concept to me. I was stepping into uncharted territory, full of trimesters, ultrasounds, and a vocabulary full of medical jargon.

For those of us used to the straightforwardness of our annual check-ups and the occasional drop-in for unexpected illnesses, prenatal visits are indeed a different experience. Here's a brief rundown of what you might expect in terms of scheduling:

- **First Trimester:** The initial prenatal visit typically happens at around eight weeks, then subsequent check-ups might run every month or so. The first visit is quite comprehensive, discussing health histories and potential risks, and often including an ultrasound to confirm the pregnancy and check on the baby's heartbeat!

- **Second Trimester:** Regular check-ups continue, often around every four weeks. Expect ultrasounds between 18 and 20 weeks, where you can likely find out the sex of the baby (if you so choose).

- **Third Trimester:** Visits become more frequent, happening every two weeks from weeks 28 through 36, then weekly until delivery. During these visits, discussions about birth plans, potential complications, and final preparations for delivery take center stage.

Of course, high-risk pregnancies may involve a different, often more frequent schedule.

During these visits, you'll be swamped with terms like blood tests, glucose levels, and various measurements. Let curiosity be your guide here—ask, ask, and ask again. Every question is a steppingstone to understanding and becoming an active participant in this journey.

Ultrasound visits are a special kind of magic! They happen less frequently, typically during the first visit, again at around 18-20 weeks, and possibly later in the third trimester to ensure everything is on track. When you see that little fluttering heartbeat on the screen, it's an ethereal experience. It's a grainy, fuzzy image that will likely be the most beautiful thing you've ever seen, eliciting emotions from places deep within you that you never realized existed.

But what is your role in all of this? It's not defined by your physical experience. You're not actually carrying the baby, but your presence, supportive hand, and focused attention do carry significance. It's how you gently hold her hand during the ultrasound, your engaged listening and active participation during the doctor's talk, and the warmth of reassurance in your eyes that silently remind her, "We're in this together."

Every action—every gentle squeeze of the hand or soft whisper of encouragement—reassures her that she's not navigating these uncharted waters alone.

Questions to Discuss with Your Partner

Communication is the cornerstone of any strong relationship, and it becomes even more critical during pregnancy. It's essential to create a space where both of you can express concerns, dreams, and even those wacky midnight ice cream cravings. Here are some questions to kick-start those deep-dive conversations:

1. How do you feel about finding out the baby's gender beforehand?

2. Are there any specific birthing plans or preferences you're leaning toward?

3. How involved do you want your families to be during the pregnancy and post-delivery?

4. What are your biggest fears or worries, and how can you help alleviate them for each other?

5. How do you envision sharing parental responsibilities once the baby arrives?

The last thing you want is to find yourself on different pages, especially when things get real. Addressing these questions early on will help you both navigate the journey with a united front.

In the sections to come, we'll dive deeper into topics like miscarriage and the importance of relaxation for Mom. But remember, the road to fatherhood is not just about gathering knowledge. It's also about immersing yourself, heart and soul, into this beautiful process, cherishing every moment, and building a strong foundation for your budding family.

Miscarriage: Addressing the Loss and Moving Forward Together

When discussing the joys and challenges of pregnancy, it's also critical to talk about the possibility of miscarriage, a topic that my friend Mark opened up about during a candid conversation we had. He shared, "It was the hardest thing we've ever gone through," unveiling the emotional and often unspoken pain that many couples face.

Let's address the statistical and medical aspects straight away. Miscarriages are, unfortunately, relatively common, occurring in about 10-20% of known pregnancies, with around 80% of these happening in the first trimester, according to the American College of Obstetricians and Gynecologists. Some research even suggests the actual number might be higher, since a miscarriage can happen before someone knows they're pregnant. Medically speaking, a miscarriage is defined as the loss of a pregnancy before the 20-week mark, while a loss between 20 and 27 weeks is classified as a stillbirth. Both scenarios present a challenging emotional journey.

Miscarriages can happen for various reasons, and sometimes the cause remains unknown, which can be particularly challenging for parents seeking answers. They are commonly attributed to chromosomal abnormalities in the fetus, issues with the placenta, or underlying health conditions of the parents. Regardless, it's crucial to remember that a miscarriage is not the fault of the parents.

Navigating the emotional aftermath of a miscarriage involves traversing a myriad of emotions—from deep sorrow and guilt to a sense of loss for the envisioned future with the unborn child. It's vital to acknowledge, express, and work through these emotions.

From Mark's subsequent conversations, it became clear that joining a support group offered a pathway toward healing for him and his wife. Connecting with others who had undergone similar despair provided a safe space to share stories, unburden their pain, and extend mutual empathy, offering a semblance of peace and gradual healing.

If you and your partner face this difficult journey, it's crucial to seek support. Finding strength in vulnerability, leaning on loved ones, professionals, and each other, and connecting with a community that understands your pain can pave the way toward healing. It's a unique journey, but one you need not walk alone.

Tired but Wired: Encouraging Rest and Relaxation for Mom

I'll never forget the time my sister called me at 2:00 AM during her third trimester, complaining about her swollen feet and her insatiable craving for pickles dipped in chocolate. Pregnancy is a wild ride, not just for moms-to-be, but for their partners and other members of their support network, too.

If there's one thing I've learned, it's that fatigue is a constant companion for pregnant women. Ironically, with so much happening inside their bodies, a peaceful night's sleep can be as elusive as that legendary sock lost in the laundry.

So, what can you do to support her during these restless nights? Consider offering a soothing foot massage. This gentle act of care not only provides some much-needed comfort for her, it also demonstrates your empathy and involvement as a partner. It's about being there for her, sharing the journey, and showing that you understand and are responsive to her needs.

Also consider investing in a comfortable pregnancy pillow. It might just become her favorite bedtime companion (don't be jealous, it's just a pillow). And don't forget the power of a well-timed nap. Sometimes, the best way to recharge is to shut off for a short while.

Above all, be patient. There might be nights when she's tossing and turning, or days when the hormones seem to have commandeered her mood. These moments can test your mettle as a partner. But with a little humor and heaps of compassion, you'll both navigate them beautifully.

I recall Mark, the same friend who experienced a miscarriage, humorously recounting his wife's pregnancy cravings. "One day, it was spicy tacos; the next, it was lemon sorbet. I felt like I was living with a very unpredictable food critic," he laughed. But underneath that jest was an underlying tone of admiration and awe for the journey they undertook together.

That's what it's all about—navigating the unexpected twists and turns, hand in hand, with love, laughter, and a shared sense of adventure.

Pampering Mom: Tips for Making Pregnancy More Comfortable

I remember an evening when my cousin Dave was meticulously setting up a foot soak station for his wife, Anna. When I asked him why, he winked and said, "Haven't you heard? A relaxed wife equals a relaxed life!"

Dave was onto something. During pregnancy, a woman's body is working overtime, creating an incredible new life. As the supporting act in this beautiful journey, it's your job to make sure she feels cared for, loved, and pampered. Here are some practical tips:

1. **Cuddle Sessions:** Remember those lazy Sunday morning cuddles, before the alarm clock of life rang? Bring them back. Physical touch releases oxytocin, the "love hormone," which can help reduce anxiety.

2. **Create a Spa at Home:** Turn your bathroom into a makeshift spa. A warm bath with some gentle music can work wonders. **Pro Tip:** Lavender essential oil can help promote relaxation.

3. **Listen Actively:** This one is more about emotional pampering. Listen to her concerns, her joys, and her oddball cravings. Sometimes, lending a listening ear is the best form of comfort you can offer.

4. **Midnight Craving Runs:** If she wakes up with a hankering for mangoes in the middle of December, make sure you are up to the

challenge. Hunting down out-of-season fruit is just part of the adventure!

Dad's Toolbox: Essential Items and Resources for a Smooth Start

Every craftsman needs his tools, and the same goes for an expectant father. I remember being so overwhelmed by all the gadgets and gizmos out there. "Do we really need a baby wipe warmer?" I'd ask.

Here's a quick list of the essentials:

1. **Dad's Book Corner:** Knowledge is power. Invest in a couple of insightful pregnancy and newborn care books. And don't worry, they're not all 500 pages long. There are some great concise reads out there, too!

2. **Support Group Contact List:** Remember, you're not alone on this journey. Keep a list of local support groups or online communities. They're great for sharing experiences and getting advice.

3. **Relaxation Tools:** Have a stash of massage oils, scented candles, and relaxing music playlists ready. You never know when you might need to create a calm environment.

4. **Humor:** Yes, humor is an essential tool, too. There will be times of stress and fatigue. Being able to share a laugh can lighten the mood and strengthen your bond.

In the spirit of humor, here's a quick anecdote. My friend, Alex, was a new dad who once remarked, "My baby's diaper has two settings: 'Peekaboo' and 'Defcon 5.' I was not prepared for the latter!" Gear up and brace yourself for those Defcon 5 moments, and remember—humor can be your secret weapon.

From a Woman's Perspective: Actionable, Practical Steps to Take

Reflecting on my first trimester, I realized there were key things that would have been helpful for my husband to know. But these insights aren't just for him; they're for every new dad out there. The first trimester comes with a lot of changes and emotions. Here are some crucial factors, and ways that you, as a new dad, can be supportive.

Emotional Turbulence: During the first trimester, your partner might experience sudden shifts in mood. One day she might be elated, feeling a deep connection to the life growing inside her, and the next day she might be overwhelmed by fears and uncertainties about the future.

- **Action Steps:** If you notice your partner experiencing these emotional highs and lows, show her your support. A comforting hug, a listening ear, and your steady presence can be incredibly reassuring. Your understanding and empathy can provide much-needed stability during these times of emotional fluctuation.

Shifting Tastes: Pregnancy can dramatically alter her sense of taste and smell. She might find that the smell of coffee, which she once loved, now makes her queasy; or, she might crave foods she never liked before.

- **Action Steps:** Adapt to these changing tastes by keeping a variety of snacks at home. Be open to changing meal plans spontaneously. Your flexibility and willingness to go with the flow will be greatly appreciated. If she complains about a food or smell, get rid of it pronto!

Physical Discomforts: The first trimester often brings fatigue and nausea. She might struggle with morning sickness or feel unusually tired throughout the day.

- **Action Steps:** Offer to give her a gentle massage or prepare a warm bath with epsom salt. These small acts of kindness can alleviate her discomfort and show her that you're attuned to her needs.

Celebrating Milestones: Prenatal checkups and ultrasounds are crucial during the first trimester. They can be moments of joy, but can also bring anxiety, as she awaits confirmation that everything is progressing well.

- **Action Step #1:** Make it a priority to attend these appointments. Consider using a shared calendar app to sync appointments and create reminder notifications. Your presence shows that you're fully involved in the pregnancy, strengthening the bond between you, your partner, and your unborn child.
- **Action Step #2:** Don't forget the milestones. There are weekly ones and monthly ones. You may not think it's significant, but she's counting every week. Share a pregnancy app with her and you'll be kept up to date with milestone notifications via email or mobile app. When she randomly asks you, "What week am I?" you won't look at her like a deer in headlights.

Understanding these aspects of the first trimester can help you, as a new dad, provide the support and empathy your partner needs.

Remember, it's about going through this journey together, adapting to changes, and being there for each other every step of the way.

Key Takeaways

As a soon-to-be dad, your role in the first trimester is crucial. Here are key takeaways to help you navigate these early stages of pregnancy effectively:

- **Adapt to New Roles:** Embrace the transition into parenthood with enthusiasm and openness. Recognize that you're stepping into a world of new experiences, responsibilities, and emotional landscapes.

- **Engage in the Journey:** Be an active participant in prenatal care. Attend doctor visits and ultrasounds with your partner, engage in meaningful discussions, and show genuine interest in the pregnancy process.

- **Communicate and Connect:** Openly discuss your thoughts, fears, and expectations about the pregnancy and the future. This strengthens your bond and ensures you both navigate the journey with a united front.

- **Provide Emotional Support:** Be sensitive to the hormonal changes and emotional swings your partner experiences. Offer reassurance, understanding, and a listening ear to help her through challenging moments.

- **Pamper and Comfort:** Recognize the physical demands of pregnancy on your partner. Offer comfort by giving massages, creating a relaxing environment, and attending to her needs and cravings.

- **Prepare for Various Outcomes:** Understand and prepare for the possibility of miscarriage. Offer support and empathy during difficult times and seek external support if needed.

- **Equip Yourself with Knowledge:** Arm yourself with information about pregnancy and childbirth. Read books, join support groups, and gather resources to better understand and support your partner.

- **Embrace the Experience with Humor and Love:** Use humor and love to navigate the journey. Understanding that pregnancy is a shared experience filled with challenges and joys will help you both build a stronger relationship and family foundation.

Embrace these guidelines to be the supportive and understanding partner your spouse needs during the first trimester. Your engagement and care will pave the way for a healthy and joyful journey into parenthood.

Chapter Two

ROCKING THE SECOND TRIMESTER: BONDING AND PREPARING (WEEKS 13-26)

"The heart of a father is the masterpiece of nature."
— *Antoine François Prévost, Manon Lescaut*

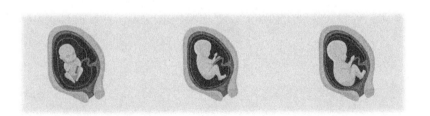

Welcome to the blissful middle, gentlemen. Picture the second trimester as the comforting bridge between the topsy-turvy onset of pregnancy and the tangible anticipation of the third trimester. If the first trimester was the thrilling climb of a roller coaster track, these middle weeks offer a stretch where you can catch your breath, gaze around, and genuinely start to enjoy the ride.

As the initial unease and uncertainties subside, this trimester offers the space for you, as an expectant dad, to truly lean in—to bond, prepare, and nurture not just the unborn child, but also the evolving relationship with your partner.

Let's start by debunking some myths. Those emotional highs and lows, the excitement, and the fears? They're not exclusive to moms. Dads, too, have a whirlwind of emotions, ranging from exhilarating joy to the daunting responsibility of upcoming fatherhood.

Have you ever caught yourself staring at that crib setup, wondering how on Earth you'll ensure your baby's best future? You're not alone. One minute you might be marveling at the sonogram, the next you're deep-diving into the best baby monitors on the market, all while battling those sneaky pangs of self-doubt. Will you be a good father? How will you balance work, personal life, and the monumental shift about to happen in your family dynamic?

The key is preparation, both practical and emotional. By the end of this chapter, you'll have a roadmap guiding you through these transformative weeks, from understanding your partner's physical changes to establishing bedtime routines for both the baby and the exhausted parents. Learn how to be an emotional rock for your partner, how to anticipate her needs, and how to weave those essential threads of connection with your soon-to-be kiddo.

From assembling that intriguing piece of baby furniture to attending prenatal classes where you learn that breathing techniques are not just for yoga, this trimester is teeming with experiences that are both enlightening and sometimes downright comical.

What's Happening to Baby and Mom - Quick Stats

In the delightful expedition that is the second trimester (sometimes known as the "honeymoon phase" of pregnancy), both Mom and Baby go through extraordinary transformations. Between weeks 13 and 26, expectant mothers often experience a burst of energy, reduced nausea, and an adorable, more pronounced baby bump. Meanwhile, within that burgeoning belly, Baby is busily crafting tiny fingers and toes, opening and closing those little eyes, and even getting startled by loud noises. Yes dads, your baby is quickly becoming a mini-human, complete with expressions, movements, and a heartbeat!

Weeks 13-15:

- **Baby:** Now about the size of a lemon, the little champ is starting to move those tiny limbs around, even if Mom can't feel it yet. Facial features are becoming more defined, and the baby can even make a fist.
- **Mom:** Many moms find that early pregnancy symptoms like nausea start to decrease. In addition, the baby bump might start

becoming noticeable to others. "Hey, are you pregnant?" might be a question they begin to hear.

Weeks 16-19:

- **Baby:** This tiny human is now the size of a mango. Its skin is still translucent, Baby might begin to hear external noises. So, go ahead and play some soothing tunes, or maybe your favorite rock band.
- **Mom:** She might start feeling some fluttering movements, often described as "butterflies" or "popcorn popping." It's the baby's first way of saying, "Hey, I'm here!"

Weeks 20-22:

- **Baby:** The baby is now the size of a small banana, and its developing senses are sharpening. Those little kicks and punches become more noticeable, and, if you're lucky, you might even see a little foot or hand pressing against the belly.
- **Mom:** As the belly grows, she might start to feel more comfortable in maternity clothes. Also, that 20-week ultrasound can often tell if you should paint the nursery pink or blue!

Weeks 23-26:

- **Baby:** Now the size of a cauliflower, the little one is becoming more proportionate. Lungs are developing, preparing for that first breath of air.
- **Mom:** She may start to feel more tired as the extra weight and baby's activity increase. A gentle reminder to the dads—foot rubs are always appreciated around this time!

Baby Bump Beauty: Celebrating the Growing Belly with Awe and Amusement

There's something magical about watching a belly grow. It's the universe's way of showing us that the best things come with time. As a first-time dad, it's natural to be fascinated by the transformation. You might find yourself constantly placing your hand on the belly, hoping for a tiny kick. It's a profound connection, knowing that your child is just inches away.

During pregnancy, your partner might have moments of self-reflection and humor about the changes her body is going through. For instance, one day she might be excited about her new maternity jeans, and the next, she might whimsically comment on how her belly button looks different. In these moments, being supportive and sharing in her light-heartedness helps strengthen your bond. It's these small, shared experiences that add warmth and joy to the journey of pregnancy.

The transformation is both awe-inspiring and amusing. There's no other experience quite like it. Whether you're taking weekly belly photos, talking to the bump every night, or dancing to quirky tunes, make sure you cherish every single moment of this journey. After all, it's not every day you get to witness the creation of life right before your eyes.

Remember, it's not just about how the belly looks, but also the world it holds within. As you progress through these weeks, take time to bond, prepare, and, most importantly, celebrate the magic that's unfolding.

What's Quickening? Baby's First Kicks

There I was, lounging on the couch after a long day, when my wife suddenly grabbed my hand and placed it on her belly. She had a wide-eyed look of wonder and said, "Did you feel that?" Confused, I squinted at her tummy as if it would start speaking to me. And then, there it was: a slight flutter, like a tiny butterfly trying to make its presence known. That, my friends, was our baby's first kick, also known as "quickening."

It's one of the most magical moments of pregnancy, both for the mom and the eagerly waiting dad. Typically felt between 18 and 25 weeks, these first movements can feel like a gentle tap, a rolling sensation, or even popcorn popping. Every baby is different, and so is every mom's description of the sensation. But rest assured, once you've felt it for the first time, you'll be eagerly awaiting the next little jig from your mini-dancer.

Eager to feel the baby, some first-time dads might press their ears to their partners' bellies, expecting a drum solo. But patience is key. If you don't feel it the first time, don't fret. There'll be plenty more performances in the upcoming weeks.

Heartburn Havoc: Conquering the Fire of Indigestion

A friend of mine once joked during his wife's pregnancy, "Our baby is going to come out with a full head of hair, considering all this heartburn she's having!" An old wives' tale suggests heartburn during pregnancy means a hairy baby. However, this is just a fun myth.

That being said, heartburn, scientifically known as acid reflux, can be a frequent, uninvited guest during the second trimester. As the baby grows, there's more pressure on the stomach, which can send stomach acid upwards, causing that uncomfortable burning sensation. So, while Mom is creating life, she might also feel like she's swallowed a small dragon.

For the dads out there, your role extends beyond just observing from the sidelines. It's about actively participating and offering comfort in simple, yet effective ways.. Here's what you can do to help:

1. **Offer Small Meals:** Encourage her to have smaller meals throughout the day. This helps reduce the pressure on the stomach.
2. **Upright Posture:** After meals, suggest a short walk or sitting upright. Gravity is your ally here.
3. **Avoid Triggers:** Some foods can exacerbate heartburn, such as spicy foods, citrus, caffeine, and chocolate.
4. **Over-the-Counter Antacids:** Check with her health care provider if it's okay for her to take these. When given the green light, keep them handy.

Remember, while heartburn can be uncomfortable, it's just another part of the journey. If heartburn really did correlate to hair growth, we'd have a world full of Rapunzels.

Side Note: Once, after a particularly spicy meal, I tried to empathize with my wife's heartburn by eating an entire chili pepper. Not only did I feel the fire, but I also got a one-hour lecture on "not everything needs a demo, hun." Stick to the antacids.

Body Image Boost: Showering Her with Compliments and Affection

In the busy days leading up to our baby's arrival, amid the endless to-do lists, two things truly mattered. First, absorbing every bit of wisdom from childbirth classes to mentally and emotionally prepare us for welcoming our new family member. And just as importantly, supporting my partner as she navigated her changing body image with kindness and empathy.

Tom, a buddy of mine, once confided, "Man, I just don't get it. My wife looks stunning with her baby bump, but she just keeps feeling down about herself. What do I do?" Tom's situation is far from unique. As pregnancy progresses, our partners' bodies undergo tremendous changes. These transformations, while vital for the baby's growth, can sometimes lead to a dip in self-esteem for expecting moms. Amidst the weight gain and physical transformations, she might not feel as confident in her appearance as before.

But here's the good news—you can help overcome this! Never underestimate the power of your words and actions. Every compliment and act of affection goes a long way. When she's standing in front of the mirror examining her body, come up from behind, wrap your arms around her, and tell her how beautiful she looks. When she feels down because her favorite dress doesn't fit anymore, surprise her with a maternity dress and a date night.

I still recall my wife's smile when I'd tell her that her glow outshone the brightest stars in the night sky. I know it sounds cheesy, but trust me, it made her day every single time. The key is to be genuine. And if you genuinely look, you'll realize she's more radiant than ever.

Childbirth Classes and Daddy Crash Courses: Gaining Knowledge and Confidence

The world of childbirth can be overwhelming. For many of us, the process might seem as complex and daunting as orchestrating a space launch. But with proper preparation, you can turn uncertainty into assurance.

Childbirth classes are an excellent resource, not just for expectant mothers, but for future fathers, as well. These sessions provide insights into several essential topics, including:

1. **The Stages of Labor:** Familiarize yourself with the different phases and what they entail.
2. **Breathing Techniques:** Due to Baby's growth and its impact on Mom's lungs, mastering effective breathing methods is crucial. These techniques are beneficial during pregnancy and indispensable during labor. Practicing together ensures both of you are in sync and that she feels wholly supported.
3. **Pain Management:** Discover both medical and non-medical pain relief options.
4. **Postpartum Care:** Grasp what the initial hours and days after delivery might entail for both mother and child.
5. **Hands-on Techniques:** Equip yourself with skills such as diaper changing, swaddling, and recognizing baby cues.

With the convenience of today's digital resources, attending these classes has never been easier. Whether you prefer live virtual sessions or pre-recorded ones available on platforms like YouTube, you can find an approach that fits your schedule.

Think of acquiring this knowledge as building a toolkit. Each piece of information and every new skill boosts your readiness for the unpredictable yet wonderful journey ahead. Completing seemingly simple tasks, like swaddling your baby or flawlessly changing a diaper, imparts a sense of pride that's hard to put into words.

The Art of Massaging: Relieving Pregnancy Pains and Stress

Jared was a pragmatic man, always firm in his belief that he could conquer any challenge with logic and rationality. That is, until his wife, Emily, entered the second trimester of her pregnancy. Suddenly, the emotional and physical shifts in her body transformed her into someone he still deeply adored, but only vaguely recognized. Every moment became an intricate dance between uncharted hormonal surges and emotional interludes. Jared's logical approach, as you might expect, was often trampled under the symphony of Emily's newly formed pregnancy needs.

After witnessing Emily's discomfort from the physical strain of pregnancy, Jared decided to introduce a gentle remedy—massage. He dove into YouTube tutorials, ensuring his hands learned the symphony of touch that could provide his beloved with comfort and reassurance. He focused on understanding the nuances of pregnancy massages, well aware that this wasn't just about physical relief, but also an intimate moment of connection between him, Emily, and the life growing within her.

Making massage a nightly routine turned into a soothing ritual for Emily and their unborn child, bringing comfort and relaxation to both. Gentle strokes on her back, tender pressure on her aching feet, and a soft hand cradling her belly—every touch was a silent promise of unwavering support.

You may discover that the physical act of providing a massage does not just bestow relief upon your partner, but also becomes a silent dialogue between you and your unborn child—a tactile whisper, bonding and forming connections that are woven into a tapestry of love and unified family. And honestly, massages aren't just for Mom. The act of nurturing and providing for her will kindle a warmth within you, forming a deeper bond that is silently communicative and beautifully heartfelt.

Mastering the Art of Back Massages and Counter-Pressure Techniques

During pregnancy, a partner's changing body means that discomfort, and especially backaches, is a constant companion. As a soon-to-be dad, this is where you can actively step in to offer support and relief. Let's take a cue from Alex, who found himself on a mission to understand and alleviate some of his pregnant partner's physical strains.

Initially, Alex focused on general back massages. Gentle rubbing and kneading on the back can provide immense relief, but paying attention to your partner's reactions and feedback is essential. Remember, the aim is not to showcase technical prowess, but to offer genuine, responsive care.

Counter-pressure techniques are an often-overlooked but invaluable tool during pregnancy. Counter-pressure involves applying a firm, steady pressure to specific areas (often the lower back) using the heel of your hand or a firm object. This pressure can help offset some of the intense pressure and pain your partner might feel during contractions or general backaches. It's almost like pushing against the pain—and for many, it's an effective way to manage it.

For Alex, integrating counter-pressure techniques required a bit more practice and communication. Determining the right amount of pressure and the most effective locations required ongoing feedback from his partner. But over time, with patience and persistence, he became adept at providing this form of relief, further connecting with his partner's experience during the pregnancy.

A little knowledge and a lot of attention can go a long way. You don't need to be a massage therapist to offer comfort. Being present and willing to learn—and listening to your partner's needs—are the most crucial components in this journey of physical and emotional support during pregnancy.

Love Notes to the Belly: Connecting with the Baby and Building a Bond

Jared soon recognized that his relationship with his unborn child didn't have to wait for its physical appearance in the world outside. He began speaking to the little one—whispering sweet nothings, singing lullabies, and often sharing stories of his day. He would lay his hand gently on Emily's belly, feeling the stirrings from within, each tiny kick a Morse code of connection between him and the baby.

He called it "Love Notes to the Belly."

It's a secret little world, where future dads create a haven of sounds and emotions that caress their babies' developing minds and souls. It's never too early to foster a connection—to let them know that there is a voice and presence that is patiently awaiting their arrival, ready to shower them with love and joy.

Perhaps you might recount tales of how you and their mom met, or the excitement and trepidations you felt upon discovering you were going to be a dad. Your voice will become a familiar comfort, anchoring them in the symphony of love that has surrounded them since conception.

It was during those moments, with his hand on Emily's belly, sharing tales of love and life with his unborn child, that Jared recognized a shift within himself, too. His connection with Emily deepened as he witnessed her glow, her laughter, and the shared secret glances that spoke of a journey only the two of them understood.

In these simple yet profound moments, Jared discovered he was unconsciously weaving a nest—one that cradled his growing family in threads of love, empathy, and connectedness. This was his silent vow, a promise whispered into the growing bump, that he would always be a harbor of safety and love for them.

The connection and bonds you form during pregnancy will be the foundation upon which you build your future as a family. Like Jared, the things you do and say, and the way you emotionally support your partner create lasting memories. These moments—from every shared look and each gentle touch to every whispered "I love you" directed at the beloved belly—are what build your family's story, which will be cherished for generations.

Prenatal Pampering: Treatments and Surprises for the Mom-to-Be

As your partner's belly becomes more noticeable, it's a clear sign that your baby will be arriving in just a few months. It's also an indication that your partner is doing a lot of heavy lifting, both figuratively and literally! As you might imagine, she can get quite tired, and a little pampering can go a long way.

Let's talk about Frank, an excited soon-to-be dad who learned that pampering isn't just for babies. Frank had always prided himself on being a considerate partner, but the second trimester opened him up to a mix of new challenges and opportunities. His partner, Eliza, found herself in a constant battle with back pain and swollen feet. Frank felt slightly helpless at first, but decided that being passive was not an option.

Frank discovered the art of prenatal pampering. He learned that the secret lay not only in grand gestures, but also in the subtle, consistent acts of love and care. He found joy in crafting small surprises for Eliza, like drawing her a warm bath infused with calming lavender oil or preparing a surprise snack of fresh fruit and yogurt.

He didn't stop there. Frank also educated himself about safe prenatal massage techniques, ensuring that his attempts to soothe Eliza's aching muscles were both effective and secure for the baby. He became an expert at creating an ambiance of tranquility in their home, using soft music, dim lighting, and the subtle fragrance of essential oils. He discovered that the gift of physical comfort, through small acts like these, also alleviated Eliza's emotional stresses, knitting a tighter bond between them.

Nurturing Your Relationship: Keeping the Love Alive During Pregnancy

While navigating this intimate journey, Frank also learned the importance of emotional connection. Your relationship, like Frank's, will undergo changes during pregnancy. The shared excitement, fears, and plans for the future bring with them a deluge of emotions, which can sometimes be quite overwhelming for both partners.

The secret here is communication—an open, honest, and heartfelt dialogue that permits vulnerability and strength to coexist harmoniously. Frank initiated conversations with Eliza about her fears, her joy, her expectations, and her needs, ensuring that she felt heard and valued. He shared his own thoughts and anxieties, too, allowing Eliza to understand his emotions.

Expressing love and admiration towards your pregnant partner, as Frank did, is of the utmost importance. He kept the spark alive through tiny love notes hidden in Eliza's lunch box, unexpected hugs from behind, and simply saying, "I love you" at spontaneous moments. This not only solidified their emotional connection, but also fostered a nourishing environment for their budding family.

You have the power to create a harmonious balance, providing a sanctuary of physical relief, emotional support, and unexpected joy for your partner during these incredible months of transformation.

It's your turn to be the pamperer, the supporter, the comedian, and, most importantly, the unwavering pillar of love and strength your partner needs.

From Dad Bod to Dad Bond: Staying Active and Fit Together

Mike was a champion napper and couch connoisseur who was suddenly thrust into the expecting dad scene. The big question for him was how to evolve from a leisure-loving individual to an engaged, active participant in shared fitness, all while maintaining his championship napping status.

For Mike, the trick was intertwining light fitness with delightful bonding experiences. His walks transformed into scavenger hunts for the ultimate ice cream spot, cleverly catering to his partner's intensified adoration for double chocolate chip delights. Yoga sessions morphed into side-splitting duo challenges, where gentle stretches became a stage for lighthearted folly and chuckles.

But beyond the laughter and sweet treats lies a salient point about the importance of exercise during pregnancy, which is the focus of this section.

The Integral Role of Exercise for Expecting Moms: Exercise, especially during pregnancy, isn't solely about maintaining physicality. It's also a crucial element for managing stress, enhancing circulation, and building endurance—all of which are vital for the pregnancy journey and the marathon of labor that awaits. As the belly grows and the physical toll becomes more evident, movement becomes both increasingly vital and progressively challenging.

The increasing weight and changing center of gravity can create a variety of physical challenges for a pregnant woman, including backaches, leg cramps, and general discomfort. Engaging in moderate, consistent exercise can alleviate some of these discomforts, offering not just physical relief, but an emotional uplift, as well.

A Joint Fitness Journey: Here's where the role of the partner becomes so important. Engaging in a shared fitness journey isn't just about the pregnant individual benefiting from the activity; it's about establishing a togetherness in the experience that lends moral and emotional support.

For Mike, embracing an active lifestyle alongside his partner meant he was not only sharing the load, but also encouraging a healthy, joyous path for them both. It wasn't necessarily about sculpting abs or clocking miles; it was about being an active, present, and supportive partner, cheering on every stretch, every stroll, and every shared giggle during their goofy yoga poses.

Pregnancy Sex: Navigating the Waves of Desire, Comfort, and Safety

Intimacy during pregnancy is a sensitive topic, and one that involves physical changes, emotions, and preserving the spark while your partner's belly grows and hormones fluctuate.

John and his wife found themselves navigating these uncharted waters with both trepidation and laughter. Their once spontaneous love life now required a few more logistics, such as negotiating the protruding belly and the often conflicting waves of desire and caution. For John, understanding, communication, and flexibility were key. Their intimate moments morphed into a gentle dance—sometimes clumsy, often exploratory, but always anchored in love and mutual respect.

Some days brought passionate connections, while others ushered in a gentle holding of hands and soft exchanges of love. John learned that maintaining intimacy was not just about the physical acts, but also being present, in-tune, and responsive to his partner's changing needs, desires, and comforts.

Addressing the Ebb and Flow of Libido During Pregnancy

The fluctuations in libido and sex drive during pregnancy is one particular area where John and his partner, like so many other couples, were treading new ground. The hormonal changes brought unexpected and sometimes perplexing variations in sexual desires.

Transparent conversations about these fluctuations were essential. It was vital for John to comprehend that an increase or decrease in his partner's sexual desire was a typical part of pregnancy and not a reflection of her feelings towards him or their relationship. John's emotions and libido were equally valid, and merited discussion to ensure both partners felt heard, appreciated, and mutually satisfied wherever possible.

Maintaining a healthy sexual relationship during pregnancy involves open dialogue, a dash of creativity, and a willingness to adapt and explore. Whether it's understanding positions that accommodate a growing belly or navigating the emotional tides that pregnancy often stirs, being present and supportive is key.

Your role is to navigate these changes with understanding and adaptability, ensuring that the physical and emotional facets of your relationship remain strong.

Exploring intimacy during pregnancy, especially as a future dad, can bring forth a mixture of emotions and questions. "Is it safe?" "Will it be awkward?" "What if I bump the baby on the head?!" Don't worry—you won't.

Let's dive into some super practical tips to keep the sparks flying, while always remaining mindful of our partners' feelings.

1. Communication

First and foremost, talking openly about desires, feelings, and apprehensions is key. Establish a clear line of communication about what's comfortable, what's desirable, and what's a no-go.

2. Position, Position, Position!

Now might be a good time for some fresh sexual choreography. Consider positions that do not put pressure on the abdomen. Many couples find that having the pregnant partner on top or in side-by-side positions can be more comfortable and enjoyable.

3. Embrace the Waves

Sexual desire during pregnancy can be fickle. Sometimes it'll skyrocket, thanks to those rampaging hormones, while at other times it may plummet. Be flexible and understanding, and explore alternative ways to be intimate, such as cuddles, gentle touches, and kisses.

4. Lubrication Station

Pregnancy can bring about changes in vaginal lubrication. Having a good-quality, water-based lubricant can lead to smoother sailing and deeper intimacy.

5. Pillow Power

Utilize pillows to provide extra comfort and support during the act. Placing a pillow under the hips or in between the knees can make certain positions more comfortable.

6. Emotional Check-in

Pregnancy emotions are like a box of chocolates—you never know what you're gonna get. Regular emotional check-ins, both before and after intimacy, help ensure that both partners are feeling cared for and heard.

7. Enjoy Non-Sexual Intimacy, Too

Remember, intimacy is not just about sex. Affection, attention, and emotional support are equally crucial in maintaining a healthy relationship during pregnancy.

8. Safety First

Ensure that sex during pregnancy is engaged in safely. In most cases, it is perfectly safe, but certain complications or risk factors might warrant some restrictions. Always consult your health care provider to get a green light.

9. Explore and Have Fun

Pregnancy is a journey, not a limitation! Exploring new ways to be intimate, trying different positions, and embracing a playful approach can deepen your connection and spice things up!

10. Postpartum Patience

Looking slightly ahead, remember that, after the baby arrives, there'll be a period where sex is off the table. During her six-week postpartum appointment, the OB may or may not give the approval to resume physical intimacy. Be patient and supportive, and utilize this time to strengthen other aspects of your relationship.

The key takeaway is to walk alongside your partner during this journey, providing a steadying hand and a warm heart, and facilitating an environment where both of you can be candid about your feelings, desires, and needs. This is an adventure, so keep the map handy, but don't be afraid to explore uncharted territories together! If ever you feel lost, revert back to tip number one: communicate!

Choosing a Baby Name: An Adventure of Compromise and Uniqueness

Naming your baby can feel like a high-stakes game. The instant you share the news of an impending arrival, a cascade of suggestions typically follows—some welcome, and others less so.

Derek was an excited future dad. He was all set with preparations for the nursery, all the way down to the diaper brand, but stumbled when it came to settling on a name. Derek gravitated towards classic options, while his wife, Lisa, leaned towards more unconventional choices. Neither seemed willing to shift their stance.

The process of choosing a baby name is a delicate balance of family tradition, individuality, and a lot of love and compromise. So, how do you traverse the sometimes tricky process of choosing names and settle on the one? Here are some practical tips that Derek and Lisa found helpful.

Practical Tips to Choose Your Baby Name

1. **Create a Shortlist:** Both partners should compile lists of their favorite names, complete with the reasons behind each choice.

2. **Meaning Matters:** Opting for a name with a specific or special meaning can add an extra layer of significance.

3. **Sound It Out:** Enunciate the name alongside your surname, being mindful of any unintended nicknames or awkward initials that might result from the combination.

4. **Family Ties:** While respecting family traditions can be heartfelt, it's also perfectly acceptable to venture outside of familial norms.

5. **Veto Power:** Each partner should have the ability to veto names they absolutely cannot envision for their child.

6. **The Public Opinion (or not):** Decide collectively whether you want to keep the chosen name under wraps or share it with others before your baby's debut.

7. **Visualize the Spelling:** When stuck between different spellings of a chosen name, write each variant out in both cursive and print. See how each version feels to write and how it looks on paper. This visual exercise can often illuminate the right choice and help you imagine what it will be like for your child to write their name in the future.

Guided by these steps, Derek and Lisa ultimately settled on "Eliana," a name that beautifully intertwined tradition and uniqueness, paying homage to their grandmothers, Elaine and Anna.

Your adventure through the name-selecting process is a journey that is shared with your partner. Though you might occasionally find yourselves at odds, the path to selecting that perfect name will undoubtedly be a memory you'll cherish—especially when you whisper that name to your new arrival.

Bracing for Braxton Hicks: The Unrehearsed Rehearsal

Let's talk about the unexpected guest of the second trimester—Braxton Hicks contractions. Lisa first experienced them during a cozy movie night. One moment she was deeply engrossed in the plot, the next, her hand was clutching Derek's, eyes wide with concern.

Braxton Hicks, often called "practice contractions," are like the body's way of rehearsing for the big show, but without the actual labor part. Here's what Derek (and all future dads) need to know:

- **Spotting Them:** They can feel like a tightening in the abdomen, but are usually not as painful as the real deal.
- **Time Them:** They're irregular and usually don't come close together.
- **Comfort Measures:** Encourage your partner to change positions or try relaxation techniques during these contractions.
- **Hydration Is Key:** Sometimes, ensuring that your partner is well-hydrated can help alleviate Braxton Hicks.

- **When to Seek Help:** If contractions are regular, painful, and/or accompanied by any other concerning symptoms, it's essential to seek medical advice pronto.

Understanding the curious case of Braxton Hicks can be a mixed bag of emotions and challenges. But fear not! With understanding, empathy, and a dash of humor, you and your partner can navigate through this exciting chapter together, forming not just a connection, but a team ready to welcome your little one into the world.

Babymoon Bliss: A Pre-Parental Getaway to Remember

A babymoon is like a honeymoon, but for soon-to-be parents. It's a sweet little vacation you take with your partner before your world turns upside down with late-night diaper changes and lullabies. Many parents-to-be use this as a way to enjoy each other's company one last time without the interruptions of a crying baby.

I remember the time I suggested a babymoon to my wife. I pitched the idea of a jungle trek in Thailand. I envisioned us trekking through the wilderness, setting up camp by the riverside, battling mosquitoes, and having the times of our lives. However, while we've always had a shared passion for hiking and exploration, the dynamics had changed with her pregnancy. She looked at me as though I'd grown a second head, laughed, and said, "Honey, I'm pregnant, not auditioning for an adventure reality show!"

When planning a babymoon, consider comfort and relaxation, not just adventure. Beach destinations, countryside retreats, or spa resorts can offer a serene environment for both of you. Additionally, ensure that clean restroom facilities are readily available whenever needed!

Pro Tip: Ensure you have a detailed chat with your health care provider about your upcoming travel plans. Given your stage of pregnancy, there may be some restrictions or recommendations to consider. It's essential to remember that many airlines have specific policies regarding flying during pregnancy, often restricting air travel after the 36th week for single pregnancies and earlier for multiples. Make sure to check your airline's guidelines and obtain a fit-to-fly certificate from your health care provider if required.

Consider potential health risks when choosing your destination, especially in areas known to be affected by the Zika virus, which poses significant risks during pregnancy. Opt for destinations with a lower risk, and always prioritize you and your baby's health first.

Don't forget about securing travel insurance that covers any pregnancy-related events. Ensure that the policy accounts for any possible needs during your trip, such as health care access, trip cancellation, or early departure due to pregnancy-related concerns.

With a dash of preparation and a sprinkle of caution, your babymoon can be a beautiful last hurrah before the arrival of your little one. Plan wisely, travel safely, and soak in the serenity with your partner.

Dad's Toolbox: Must-Have Items for a Smooth Second Trimester

Gentlemen, this isn't your ordinary tool belt. No hammers, no nails, just essential items that will make you a superhero during the second trimester. Here's what you need:

1. **Pregnancy Pillow:** If you haven't already, invest in a good-quality pregnancy pillow for your partner. Trust me, she'll thank you.

2. **Nutritious Snacks:** No, I'm not talking about the chocolate-covered pretzels you hide at the back of the pantry. Think nuts, fruits, and yogurt. When those sudden hunger pangs strike, you'll be ready.

3. **Comfortable Footwear for Her:** Swollen feet can be a real pain—literally. Surprise your partner with comfy shoes or slippers that provide ample support. Crocs have recently gained popularity with pregnant women, as they can comfortably fit wider feet.

4. **Pregnancy Apps:** These apps can be a game-changer. They provide weekly updates about the baby's development, tips, and a platform where both of you can log your experiences. Some even have cool features, like playing sounds to the belly!

5. **Massage Oils:** This is perfect for those days when her back or feet hurt more than usual. It's also a great bonding activity!

6. **Camera:** Document all of the moments. One day, you'll look back at these photos and marvel at this incredible journey you both undertook together.

7. **Support Belt:** This helps alleviate some of the lower back pain associated with pregnancy.

Remember, the second trimester is exciting, but it can also be challenging. With this toolbox in hand, you won't just survive it; you'll ace it.

From a Woman's Perspective: Actionable, Practical Steps to Take

As we sail through the second trimester, I find myself reflecting on the nuances of this journey. There are certain things I wish my husband knew more intuitively, things that would have made this phase a bit smoother for both of us. These insights may be helpful in understanding and supporting your partner during this period.

Handling the Emotional Swings: The second trimester can present a complex mix of emotions for your partner. She might experience sudden bursts of happiness, followed by moments of worry or frustration. These feelings often stem from hormonal changes or concerns about future responsibilities and changes.

- **Action Steps:** Be ready to ride these waves with empathy and let go of any hint of judgment. When emotions fluctuate, your support means the world. A comforting hug, a listening ear, or even a shared laugh can provide the stability and reassurance your partner needs during these tricky times.

Fluctuating Energy Levels: Even if she appears more energetic, remember that growing a baby is an exhausting process. Some days, she may have a surge of energy, and on others, she may need more rest than usual.

- **Action Steps:** Encourage and participate in restful moments. Whether it's a short nap or just a quiet evening, your understanding and willingness to slow down are comforting.

Navigating Bodily Changes: As her body changes to accommodate the growing baby, these transformations can be both amazing and challenging for her to adapt to.

- **Action Steps:** Show appreciation for these changes and understand their impact on her. A spontaneous compliment, a gentle touch, or just acknowledging the amazing work her body is doing can make her feel loved and supported.

Planning for the Baby: As the baby's arrival gets closer, you'll find yourselves engaged in more preparations, from setting up the nursery to discussing how you'll handle various parenting situations.

- **Action Steps:** Be an active participant in these preparations. Engage in discussions about the nursery, parenting, and other future plans. Your involvement shows that you're equally invested in your baby's future.

This trimester is a unique and special time. By being an involved, loving, and supportive partner, you contribute to making this experience beautiful and fulfilling for both of you.

Key Takeaways

Navigating the second trimester as a soon-to-be dad involves understanding and supporting your partner's unique needs. Here are the essential actions to enhance this journey:

- **Support Emotional Changes:** Recognize and support the emotional ups and downs your partner experiences during this trimester. Be ready to offer comfort, a listening ear, and a supportive presence.

- **Stay Engaged and Informed:** Actively participate in prenatal classes and doctor's visits. Understand the physical and emotional changes that are happening and be a knowledgeable part of the pregnancy journey.

- **Maintain Intimacy:** Adapt to changes in physical intimacy. Communicate openly about comfort levels and desires, and find new ways to maintain a close bond.

- **Prepare for Parenthood Together:** Use this time for collaborative planning and decision-making, like choosing a baby name. Engage in discussions about your future as parents and share responsibilities as you prepare.

- **Prioritize Her Comfort:** Be proactive in ensuring your partner's comfort. Offer massages, help with managing heartburn, and provide emotional support.

- **Foster a Healthy Lifestyle:** Encourage and participate in light fitness activities together. This promotes not only physical health, but also emotional well-being.

- **Plan a Relaxing Babymoon:** Organize a babymoon that focuses on relaxation and quality time together. Ensure it's safe and comfortable for your pregnant partner.

- **Understand Braxton Hicks Contractions:** Learn to identify Braxton Hicks contractions and know how to provide comfort during these moments.

- **Equip Yourself with Necessary Tools:** Gather essential items, like pregnancy pillows, nutritious snacks, and comfortable footwear, to support your partner's comfort.

- **Document the Journey:** Capture this special time through photos and shared experiences, creating lasting memories of your pregnancy journey.

Embrace these strategies to effectively support and connect with your partner during the second trimester. Your active involvement and understanding will significantly contribute to a positive and memorable pregnancy experience.

Chapter Three

THRIVING IN THE THIRD TRIMESTER: NESTING, PREPPING, PLANNING, AND NERVOUS SWEATING

"Preparing for a baby is a sprint and a marathon, all in one; with each step forward, build the nest with love, stitch the plans with care, and let the nervous sweat be the sweet dew of your impending joy."
— *Alexi Panos, inspirational speaker, and author*

Welcome to the third trimester, the final stretch before you meet your little one. If you thought the second trimester was a whirlwind, strap in, because this last part is like the big climax in a movie. Everything's speeding up, and the nerves are real.

The third trimester is a mix of getting stuff done and just trying to keep up. Your partner's belly is growing, the baby's kicks are getting stronger, and, suddenly, reality sinks in: A tiny human is about to join your world. Don't worry if you're feeling a bit lost or nervous. That's perfectly normal. Heck, if there's one thing every first-time dad feels, it's a mix of excitement and "Oh, what have I gotten myself into?"

In this chapter, we'll dive into everything from setting up the nursery to understanding those intense feelings both you and your partner might be experiencing. Plus, we'll touch upon the slightly sweaty sense of nervousness that's totally okay to feel.

This part of the journey is about getting ready, both mentally and physically. While it might seem like a lot, every step you take is a step closer to one of the greatest adventures of your life. Take a deep breath and let's discuss how to make the most of these final months before you get to say, "Hello!" to your baby.

What's Happening to Baby and Mom - Quick Stats

First things first, let's take a quick look at what's going on in the world of your partner's belly. It's an exciting time for the little one, and, of course, for the mom!

Weeks 27-30:

- **Baby:** Weighs about 2 to 2.5 pounds, and can blink those tiny eyes. Might be practicing some fancy moves, too.
- **Mom:** Feeling the weight, and might start waddling. (It's cute, I promise!)

Weeks 31-33:

- **Baby:** Developing stronger bones and can hear you now! Time for those lullabies.
- **Mom:** Belly button might pop out, and the backaches and knee aches hit with a vengeance!

Weeks 34-36:

- **Baby:** Piling on weight, and the skin is smoothing out.
- **Mom:** Breathing gets tougher; baby's getting bigger!

Weeks 38-40:

- **Baby:** Ready to meet the world! Fully developed and looking for that exit door.
- **Mom:** Might be feeling real contractions. It's go-time soon!

Weeks 41+:

- **Baby:** Where's the exit? Overstaying its welcome, but will come out when ready.
- **Mom:** Anxious and probably tired of being pregnant. Patience is a virtue.

Nesting 101: Creating a Cozy & Safe Haven for Your Growing Family

Have you ever encountered the term "nesting" in the context of pregnancy? It might conjure up images of birds meticulously arranging twigs, feathers, and whatever else they can find to create a safe space for their eggs. Human nesting isn't altogether different, though it involves fewer twigs and more crib assembly.

Nesting refers to an instinctual urge that often kicks in for pregnant individuals, typically around the fifth month of pregnancy—but it can occur at any time. It emanates from a primal desire to create a secure and welcoming environment for the soon-to-be-arriving new family member. For some, it might manifest as a surge of energy and a compelling drive to organize, clean, and decorate. It's a fascinating blend of anticipation, maternal instinct, and proactive planning, where the soon-to-be-parents don't just invest in a physical space, but also emotionally prepare for the impending arrival.

Given this context, let's look at some nesting principles:

1. **Prioritize Safety:** No matter how cute that crib looks, safety comes first. Look for sturdy furniture and secure it to the walls.
2. **Pick a Theme:** Maybe you're into nautical or space, or maybe a jungle vibe. Picking a theme can make things fun and give you direction.
3. **Get Organized:** Storage, storage, and more storage! Trust me, tiny humans have a ton of stuff.
4. **Lighting Matters:** Soft lights for midnight feedings or a quick diaper change can be a lifesaver. Switch to dimmable lights. Bonus: They won't wake up your partner.

5. **Comfort Is Key:** This is true for both Baby and parents. Comfy rocking chair? Check. Easy-to-reach diaper station? Double check.

6. **Sound Proofing:** Consider a white noise machine or soft lullabies—not just for Baby, but also to drown out your occasional clumsy loudness in the middle of the night.

I remember setting up my little one's room. At one point, I ended up inside the crib, testing its sturdiness. It wasn't my proudest moment, but hey, it's all about ensuring safety, right? If you end up with a little paint on your face or a misassembled diaper station, remember, it's all part of the adventure!

This journey is as thrilling as it is nerve-wracking, and it's filled with moments you'll cherish. Every paint stroke, every piece of furniture, and even the little accidents along the way will be stories for the ages. So, dive into it with passion, laughter, and maybe a little bit of nervous sweating.

Dad's Guide to Babyproofing: Wrangling Wires and Taming Tippy Furniture

Babyproofing your home is an essential step in creating a safe environment for your little one. It's more than just socket covers and door latches; it's about transforming your space into a secure playground for exploration and growth. Here's a quick list to get you started:

1. **Secure Wires and Cords:** Use cord organizers (velcro strips, zip ties, or hair ties) to keep them out of reach.

2. **Anchor Heavy Furniture:** Furniture straps are vital to prevent tipping.

3. **Corner Protectors:** Cut and pad corners with soft materials like sponges or foam to soften sharp edges. Silicone corner pieces with adhesive backings are easy fixes, too.

4. **Drawer Locks:** Place a rubber band around paired cabinet knobs or handles to restrict opening.

5. **Carabiner Cupboard Locks:** Use carabiners to latch cupboard handles together, making it more difficult for a baby to open them.

6. **Window Safety:** Employ guards and locks against falls.

7. **Non-Slip Mats:** Essential for wet areas like the bathroom and kitchen.

8. **Toilet Locks:** Prevent unwanted water exploration.

9. **Door Knob Covers:** Control access to certain areas. Use door lever locks if you don't have knobs.

10. **Outlet Covers:** Use duct tape or plastic caps to cover electrical outlets securely.

11. **Curtain Cord Management:** Bundle and secure curtain cords with zip ties to prevent them from dangling within reach.

12. **Rugs:** Use double-sided tape to secure rugs to the floor and prevent tripping hazards.

13. **Tablecloth Security:** Secure the tablecloth to the table with binder clips to prevent your baby from pulling it off.

14. **Safety Gates:** Block stairs and risky areas. You can also connect large cardboard boxes to create a makeshift gate.

15. **Bathtub Spout Cushions:** Protect from bath time bumps.

For a more detailed list of baby proofing tips and hacks, don't forget to check our "Survival Checklists." There's a bonus page at the front of the book with instructions on how to access it. Remember, baby proofing is an ongoing process that adapts as your baby grows and explores.

Create a Care Plan for You and Mom: Surviving (and Thriving) in Month One

Once the nesting dust settles and your newborn is cradled in your arms, reality can hit like a freight train. There will be endless feeding sessions and diaper changes, coupled with the screams of a tiny human at ungodly hours. Ah, the unparalleled joys of parenting!

How Can We Make This Easier?

Creating a care plan isn't just about the logistics—it's also a mental and emotional compass during those blurry, sleep-deprived first weeks. Here's what worked for us and many others:

- **Divide and Conquer:** Assign tasks between you and your partner. Who's on diaper duty? Who's managing nighttime feedings? Do you have a strategy for who gets to sleep when?
- **Meals on Wheels (or in the Freezer):** Stock up on easy-to-cook or pre-cooked meals. Better yet, have a snack station in your room for those midnight hunger pangs that Mom will surely have if she's breastfeeding.
- **Pet Protocol:** If you have pets, they'll need some adjusting, too. Allocate time for walks and affection, ensuring they don't feel neglected amid the new changes.

Becoming a parent doesn't come with a magic wand that suddenly gives you all the knowledge you need. But with some pre-planning, a dash of elbow grease, and a heap of patience, you can create a safe and loving environment for your new family.

Choosing a Pediatrician: It's not Just for the Kiddo, It's for You, Too!

When your baby arrives in this world, he or she will need a friendly pediatrician. Selecting a pediatrician before the birth might feel like you're putting the cart before the horse, but trust me, you're going to appreciate having them ready.

When picking a pediatrician, here are a few things to consider:

- How close is their office?
- Do they accept your insurance?
- What's their personality like? (Yes, you want to like them, it makes a difference!)
- Where do they stand on topics that are important to you?
- How accessible are they outside of appointments?
- Do they reply to emails?

Visit a few offices, talk to the doctors, and get a feel for how they do things. Some will allow you to schedule "meet and greet" visits before the baby is born. You'll be visiting this person often, so make sure you and your partner are comfortable with them.

Planning for Babysitting and Daycare

Getting ready for a newborn includes planning for those moments when you're going to need some extra hands. There will be times when you crave a simple, uninterrupted shower or—dare we dream—a quiet cup of coffee. Laying the groundwork for babysitting and daycare ahead of time can help make that dream a reality.

Babies are like little celebrities—everyone wants to hold them, cuddle them, and shower them with love. But, unlike celebrities, they don't come with an entourage to manage their daily affairs! That's where you, super dad, come in, managing the assistants (babysitters and daycare).

1. Build Your Baby Squad

Your baby squad can include grandparents, uncles, aunts, or close friends who are experienced and trustworthy. These are people who would love to spend a few hours with your little one so you can snatch a bit of leisure time. Establish a rotating schedule, if possible, so you're not leaning too heavily on one person.

Pro Tip: When they're taking care of your little munchkin, try not to hover. Take that time for yourself, or spend it with your partner. They've got this, and you deserve a breather!

2. Hunting for Daycare

A good daycare is like a hidden gem, so you'll want to start searching for it pretty early on. During your search, consider factors like proximity, cost, and the overall vibe of the place. Remember, it's not just about their reputation, but also how you and your partner feel about it.

Begin your visits a few months before you think you might need them, and remember to peek into the various nooks and crannies during your tour. Ask yourself:

- Are the caregivers attentive and warm?
- Is the place clean and safe?
- How do they handle emergencies?

Most importantly, check if there's a waitlist. Many daycares have them, and you don't want to find the perfect place, only to realize there's a year-long queue.

3. Casual Babysitting

For those times when family isn't available, having a casual babysitter can be a lifesaver. Websites and apps can connect you to vetted, local babysitters. Still, it is always a good idea to interview them and check their references. Perhaps even have them over for a trial run while you're at home.

Another neat option is to form a babysitting co-op with other parents in your neighborhood. Swap babysitting nights, and voila! You have yourself a cost-effective, community-based solution.

4. Ensuring Consistency

Babies love routine, so whichever care route you choose, try to keep it consistent. Dependable caregivers, consistent timing, and a stable environment help your baby feel secure and simplify your life a smidgen in the chaotic world of parenthood.

Planning for babysitting and daycare isn't just about taking a break (although that's super important, too!). It's about creating a balanced, wholesome environment for your baby, while also caring for your own well-being. After all, happy parents equal a happy baby!

Birth Plans and Expectations: Supporting Her Choices Like a Pro

A birth plan can make the difference between a chaotic birthing experience...and a slightly less chaotic one. Think of it as a roadmap, outlining the desires and preferences of the expectant mother during labor and delivery. Whether it involves opting for an epidural, declining one, or ensuring immediate skin-to-skin contact, the details matter.

Your role in this is to stand firm as her advocate. There might come a point when she's so overwhelmed or exhausted that articulating her preferences becomes a challenge. In such moments, you become her spokesperson, ensuring that her wishes are honored. But be prepared: Childbirth is predictably unpredictable. While we all love to have plans, sometimes unforeseen complications necessitate swift decisions, some of which might never have been discussed before. It's crucial to remain adaptable, make informed choices as a united front, and always prioritize her well-being and that of the baby.

I recall the flurry of emotions and activity in the delivery room, witnessing my partner endure her labor. Though we entered armed with a birth plan, there were moments when we needed to adjust with the circumstances. Faced with unanticipated choices, I held her hand and we charted the best course forward. This is what partnership is all about—standing strong together when faced with the unexpected.

Always respect and uphold the choices made, as they lay the foundation for your growing family. In those pivotal moments, be an unwavering pillar she can lean on. One day, you'll reminisce about this time as a testament to your strength as a team.

Remember, it's not just about planning, but also taking decisive action. By offering steadfast support and anticipating the initial challenges of parenthood, you ensure a smoother transition. The proactive steps taken today will make a world of difference in the exhilarating early days of welcoming your newborn.

Hospital Tour & Logistics: "Where's the Entrance, Again?"

If you think all those folks zipping about in *Grey's Anatomy* knew their way around the hospital on day one, you're sorely mistaken. Hospitals can be labyrinthine, so consider doing a little reconnaissance before D-Day.

Find out where to park, which entrance to use, and where the maternity ward is. You want to be the guy who knows his way around when the contractions are four minutes apart, not the one asking for directions while your partner is mid-contraction.

I remember the day my cousin, Jake, mistakenly took a wrong turn with his wife, Lisa, who was having contractions. They ended up in the hospital's staff lounge, much to the amusement of a group of nurses on their break.

Here's your homework, dads: Schedule a hospital tour. They'll walk you through all the important spots and give you information on where you'll be spending those first exciting hours of your child's life.

Practice Run: "Vroom Vroom, but Safely"

Doing a dry run to the hospital isn't about seeing how fast you can make the drive (remember, safety first!). It's about knowing the route like the back of your hand, even if you're groggy at 3:00 AM. Take note of gas stations along the way, and perhaps a 24-hour coffee spot—trust me, you'll thank yourself later.

Consider doing the run at different times of the day to gauge traffic patterns, and explore alternative routes just in case your main one is blocked for some pesky reason.

The Hospital Bag: "Did We Pack the Kitchen Sink?"

Before we dive into the packing frenzy, there's good news for you. We've prepared a downloadable hospital checklist for each of you— Dad, Mom, and Baby—because yes, you each get a bag. The checklists are meticulously curated to ensure nothing essential gets left behind. Be sure to check out the link at the start of the book to access these checklists.

Let's talk about packing. This hopefully won't be a weekend trip, but you do need to pack a few essentials. First, your partner's bag. Remember to pack comfy pajamas, snacks, a going-home outfit for her and the baby, and any specific items that'll make her more comfortable.

Your bag is all about comfort and utility: snacks, toiletries, a change of clothes, and perhaps a pillow. Hospitals provide them, but if you're particular about where you lay your head, bring your own.

Don't forget the charger! Your phone will be buzzing with well-wishes, and you may want to use your camera for those first precious moments.

Pro Tip: Pack a separate "first 24 hours" bag so you're not rummaging through your suitcase looking for some obscure item while your partner is in labor.

First 24 Hours Bag Essentials:

- **Important Documents:** ID, insurance info, hospital forms.
- **Birth Plan:** A copy for easy reference.
- **Mom's Comfort Items:** Robe/nightgown, slippers, nursing bra.
- **Snacks and Water Bottle:** To stay energized and hydrated.
- **Basic Toiletries:** Toothbrush, toothpaste, deodorant, face wipes.
- **Phone Charger and Power Bank:** Keep your devices powered up.
- **Baby's First Outfit:** Onesie, socks, and hat.
- **Lip Balm for Mom:** A small but important comfort item.

In addition to the essentials, pack something tiny that's a nod to this monumental step you're both taking. It could be a letter to your partner, a tiny pair of socks for your baby, or a family photo—something to remind you of the beautiful journey ahead, even in the middle of the hospital chaos.

Remember, the trip to the hospital marks the home stretch of this incredible journey to meet the little one you've been waiting for. The anxiety, excitement, and "Oh boy, is this really happening?" is all part of the experience. Breathe—you've got this. And when it all gets to be a bit much, glance at that sentimental item you packed. It's a gentle reminder that, at the end of this, you get to say hello to your newest family member.

The Final Countdown: Anticipating Baby's Grand Entrance

The last leg of the pregnancy journey can feel a bit like that unnerving moment in a movie where the hero has to disarm a bomb. Red wire or blue wire? Or, in our case, diaper bag or hospital bag? Epidural or no epidural? Don't panic. Just breathe and stay present in the moment.

I remember a buddy of mine, Mark. He was a first-time dad, like many of you. Despite his usually unshakable demeanor, Mark would often pace up and down the hallway in his house in the lead-up to D-Day . It wasn't just the impending responsibilities that had him nervous; it was that *big unknown.*

You're not alone if you're lying in bed at night, staring at the ceiling, wondering if you'll be a good dad, or if you'll faint in the delivery room—or worse, if you'll say the wrong thing and end up sleeping on the couch. The trick is to keep things simple and straightforward.

1. **Accept the Anxiety:** Nerves? Yep, you'll have them. Instead of seeing anxiety as an enemy, view it as a sign of your deep care and investment in the well-being of your partner and baby. Every soon-to-be-dad feels it. It's a part of the package.
2. **Communication Is Key:** Talk with your partner. And when you do, really listen. Sometimes, it's not about fixing things, but

about understanding. Share your feelings, and let her share hers. You'll be surprised at how just talking it out can lighten the load.

3. **Stay Busy, but not Too Busy:** Dive into some last-minute preparations, but don't bury yourself in tasks to avoid your feelings. Balance is the name of the game. For instance, go ahead and put together that rocker that's been sitting in a box for weeks. But if you find yourself alphabetizing baby socks by color and day of the week, maybe take a step back.

4. **Learn the Basics:** Instead of mindlessly scrolling through social media, watch a quick YouTube video on diaper changing or baby swaddling. Trust me, when the time comes, you'll be glad you did.

5. **Seek Out Fellow Dads:** If Mark had talked to other dads sooner, he might have realized he wasn't alone in his hallway pacing. Sharing stories, laughing over common blunders, and getting advice from those who've been there can be a game changer.

6. **Stay Active:** Go for a walk, hit the gym, or just take a few moments to breathe deeply. This not only helps reduce stress, but also keeps you energized and ready for what's ahead.

Dad's Toolbox: Must-Have Items for Setting up the Nursery

You know that feeling when you're watching a movie and the main character is about to enter a big showdown? The montage begins, the superhero suits up, the detective gathers crucial evidence, the dad...assembles a crib? Yep, that's right! This is your time to shine, future dad! Setting up the nursery is like prepping for your own action scene. If you're looking for a foolproof way to ensure you're on top of things, be sure to get our downloadable checklist! It's detailed and ready to assist you in this adventure. So, what's in the dad-to-be toolkit for nursery prep? Let's find out.

1. **A Reliable Tape Measure:** Before you buy anything or start moving furniture, it is important to know the size of the room. Measure twice and buy once, my friend. You don't want to be that guy with a crib half hanging out the window because it didn't fit.

2. **Quality Paint and Brushes:** If you're looking to change the wall color, get low-fume paint. And remember, soft colors are easy on the baby's eyes—and yours, during those 2:00 AM feedings.

3. **Crib and Assembly Tools:** IKEA might make it look easy, but let's be honest—sometimes putting together furniture feels like you're trying to decode a secret language. Have a set of screwdrivers, wrenches, and maybe a rubber mallet on standby. And if you're like me and find a leftover screw after the whole thing is assembled, take a deep breath and start again.

4. **A White Noise Machine:** Some parents swear by this. It mimics the sounds babies hear in the womb, making the transition to the outside world a little easier.

5. **Changing Table with Storage:** You'll change more diapers than you can count, so get a sturdy changing table. Make sure there's room to store diapers, wipes, and that magic baby butt cream that will save your sanity.

6. **Diaper Pail:** Your regular trash can isn't ready for the "treasures" your baby will produce. Trust me on this one.

7. **Soft Lighting:** No one likes bright lights when they're sleepy, especially not babies. Get dimmable lights, lamps, or nightlights. It helps during those nighttime check-ins.

8. **Rocking Chair or Glider:** This is where you'll spend more hours than you can imagine, rocking, feeding, or just staring in wonder at the tiny human you helped create.

9. **Storage Baskets and Organizers:** Babies are tiny, but they come with a lot of stuff. Baskets will be your best friend.

10. **Safety Gear:** Outlet covers, cabinet locks, and edge bumpers might not be needed right away, but it's good to have them on hand for when your little one becomes mobile.

From a Woman's Perspective: Actionable, Practical Steps to Take

As you enter the final stretch of your pregnancy, there are several insights and experiences I want to share with you that I wish my partner had been privy to. The third trimester is a time of intense preparation, emotional shifts, and physical changes. While my reflections stem from our journey, they're valuable for all soon-to-be dads. Understanding these aspects is crucial for providing the right support during this critical phase.

Understanding Nesting Urges: The third trimester often triggers a nesting instinct, where she feels an urge to organize and prepare the home for the baby. This could involve rearranging furniture, deep cleaning, or setting up the nursery.

- **Action Steps:** Recognize that nesting is a profound instinct for many pregnant women. Offer your assistance, be patient with the changes, and engage actively in this process. Your involvement and understanding will make it a shared experience.

Navigating Emotional Changes: She may experience a roller coaster of emotions, ranging from immense joy to sudden anxiety. These feelings can change rapidly and are influenced by hormonal shifts and the impending arrival of your baby.

- **Action Steps:** Be a steady source of emotional support. Offer a comforting presence, listen actively, and be understanding.

Recognizing these mood swings as a normal part of pregnancy will help you provide the necessary support and stability.

Responding to Baby's Movements: She is highly attuned to the baby's movements inside her. While this is often a source of joy, it can also trigger worries, especially if there are changes in the pattern or frequency of movement.

- **Action Steps:** Share in the excitement of the baby's movements. Show interest and participate in feeling the kicks. When worries arise, be reassuring and offer to discuss any concerns with the health care provider, if needed.

Dealing with Sleep Disturbances: The growing baby and physical discomforts can lead to frequent sleep disturbances. She might struggle to find comfortable sleeping positions or wake up often during the night.

- **Action Steps:** Be understanding of these sleep challenges. Offer to help find comfortable sleeping positions, and be willing to talk or provide comfort during these restless nights.

Understanding the Birth Plan: She's likely spent time considering her birth preferences, but also understands the need for flexibility due to the unpredictable nature of childbirth.

- **Action Steps:** Familiarize yourself with the birth plan and be ready to advocate for her preferences during labor. Also, be prepared to support any necessary changes to the plan, understanding that flexibility can be crucial during childbirth.

These insights are key for new dads to understand the complexities and nuances of the third trimester. Your support, empathy, and active participation are vital during this time, helping to strengthen your relationship and prepare both of you for the arrival of your child.

Key Takeaways

The final days before your baby's arrival are a mix of preparation and patience. Here's a practical guide to navigating these moments:

- **The Final Countdown:** Keep track of any last-minute items you need to pack for the hospital. Double-check your list and ensure everything is ready to go, especially essentials like the car seat.
- **A Spectrum of Emotions:** Acknowledge your feelings. It's okay to feel nervous or overwhelmed. Discuss your anxieties with your partner or a friend, and consider practicing relaxation techniques.
- **The Arrival:** Familiarize yourself with the route to the hospital, and have a backup plan in place. Make sure you know where to park and where the maternity ward is located to minimize stress on the big day.
- **The Essence of Fatherhood:** Read up on newborn care basics and prepare to be involved from day one. Changing diapers, swaddling, and supporting your partner are practical skills that will bond you with your baby.
- **Prepare for the Journey:** Make sure your phone is charged, your camera is ready, and you have a list of people to call or message with the good news. These practical steps ensure you won't miss a beat when the action starts.

You're about to embark on a great adventure. Staying practical, informed, and prepared will help you enjoy the arrival of your new baby and step confidently into fatherhood.

Chapter Four

ANNOUNCEMENTS, SHOWERS, AND UNSOLICITED ADVICE: NAVIGATING THE SOCIAL SCENE

"Embrace the joy, navigate the chaos, and always remember:
The greatest adventures begin with the unexpected."

— *Alex Thompson*

Telling folks about your impending parenthood is a monumental step. From that adorable announcement that gets all the "Awwws" on social media to being knee-deep in baby gift wrapping, this is a time filled with excitement, joy, and a decent amount of awkwardness.

While navigating the emotions, cute baby onesies, and pile of advice that's about to come your way, it's essential to find your own path—one that respects the advice-givers, while also holding true to your own values and plans for your growing family.

Breaking the News: Fun and Creative Ways to Share the Pregnancy Announcement

Managing the social scene of pregnancy, especially announcements, can often feel like deciphering an ancient code. Every first-time dad, with his eager eyes and slightly nervous twitch, has stood where you stand, wondering how to shout from the rooftops that they're expecting—without actually having to climb up onto a roof. Announcing the exciting news can be thrilling, yet also a bit nerve-wracking, given that, for many people, it's a once-in-a-lifetime event.

When my wife and I found out we were expecting, we were over the moon and eager to share the news. However, announcing your entry into parenthood requires a thoughtful approach. It's about finding the right time, the right words, and the right way to share this significant life update with your loved ones. Here are some simple ways to share your big news:

1. The Classic "Guess What" T-shirt Trick

Imagine walking into a family gathering with a cheeky grin and a t-shirt that screams "Promoted to Daddy!" Watch as the room erupts into chaotic joy, some people maybe even rubbing their eyes, thinking they misread the shirt. It's a simple, low-effort, overwhelmingly heartwarming way to let the cat out of the bag.

2. Customized Puzzle Pieces - A Fitting Surprise

Imagine sending out regular-looking invites for a casual get-together, then, when everyone arrives, they're handed a puzzle piece. Curiosity takes over the room. As the pieces interlock, revealing a sweet message or maybe a picture of the first baby scan, the penny drops. Eyes widen, gasps echo, and tears of joy start to flow.

3. Movie Poster Reveal

Everyone loves a good movie night, so why not create a movie poster featuring you and your partner with a catchy title like "Coming Soon: Baby (Your Last Name)" and a release date? Present it in a frame or maybe roll it down dramatically before the movie starts. The applause and whistles will rival any blockbuster premiere.

4. Balloon in a Box - A Pop of Joy

Another idea is to present a beautifully wrapped box to your loved ones. The moment they open the box, a balloon floats up, revealing your message. The sheer simplicity of this heart-tugging reveal can turn any regular day into an unforgettable memory.

5. Time-Lapse Video - Grow with You

If you've documented the journey so far, a time-lapse video of your partner's growing belly—set to a touching melody, with a soft announcement towards the end—can be a real tearjerker. Watching the subtle changes, the growth, and the love that has blossomed during these initial months could be a beautiful, intimate share that welcomes your loved ones into this wonderful journey.

No Right or Wrong Way

There's no universal "right" way to announce a pregnancy. It's your news, so it should be shared in your way. When my wife and I decided to break our big news, we used a heartfelt letter to inform our parents and a fun social media post for our broader circle, but that's just one way to do it.

When it came to telling my mother-in-law, my wife took a slightly more playful route. She taped the four-piece sonogram pictures to the inside of a dessert container and hinted, "It's a special dessert. Maddox helped me make it." In her excitement for what she thought was a "surprise dessert," my mother-in-law initially missed the sonogram. With a grin, I quickly closed the lid and let her open it again, so the sonogram could be viewed properly. And to capture the priceless moment, I discreetly placed my camera in position to video record her reaction.

Being mindful of your audience and thinking about how they might react will naturally influence your announcement approach. Whether you go for sentimentality or a touch of dramatic flair, make sure it's something that resonates with both of you. Your joy will undoubtedly touch everyone who hears the news.

While emotions and unsolicited advice (brace yourself for plenty of that!) may swirl around you, always remember that your authenticity and shared happiness are what truly count in these announcements. It's a celebration, not a performance.

The Baby Registry Dilemma: Navigating the Sea of Baby Products

When I first found out I was going to be a dad, I thought, "How hard can this baby shopping thing be? Grab a crib, some diapers, and a few cute onesies, and we're set!" Little did I know that stepping into a baby store felt like being thrown into a whirlpool of strollers, gadgets, and toys that make sounds I didn't even know existed. Luckily, this guide can help you sort through the riff raff and ensure you have everything you need—and nothing you don't. Let's dive in and tackle this sea of baby products together.

1. Baby Registry Basics: You might be wondering, "Why do I need a baby registry?" It's simple: People want to buy you stuff. Your mom, her mom, that random guy from the office who loves babies—they all want to shower you with gifts. A registry helps you control the chaos and ensures you get what you need. Bonus: With many registries, you'll receive a special discount and a delightful bag filled with samples and complimentary goodies.

2. Seek Out Seasoned Parents: Before you go scanning everything in sight, have a chat with parents who've been through the wringer—who've had diaper blowouts at 3:00 AM and dealt with teething nightmares. They'll give you the lowdown on what you genuinely need. My buddy Mike, who recently became a dad, will tell you,

"Man, that wipe warmer? Best thing ever!" He'll also say, "Why did I get 50 blankets?!" Let Mike's experience and missteps be your guide.

3. Prioritize the Big Stuff: Sure, that toy that plays lullabies from around the world might sound fancy, but first it is best to focus on the big-ticket items: crib, stroller, car seat. These are the things you'll use daily, and you'll want to ensure you get the best fit for your lifestyle. Are you a jogger? Get a jogging stroller. Live in a two-story? Maybe invest in two changing tables, or a portable option.

4. Don't Fall for the Gimmicks: You'll inevitably come across items that make you think, "Wow, I definitely need that!" But do you? Do you really need a pacifier with a built-in GPS tracker? Probably not.

5. Remember, It's Okay to Make Changes: No one gets it perfect the first time. If you find that a product isn't working out, it's okay to switch it up. Remember, this is all a learning process. You're getting to know your baby and their unique needs.

Your baby registry isn't just a list; it's a battle plan. It's your first step into the dad arena, and with the right prep, you'll come out looking like a champ. Remember, it's not about having all the stuff; it's about being prepared for your new role.

Baby Shower Mania: What's the Big Deal?

Back in my day, baby showers were mainly a "women only" event. They were special gatherings where the soon-to-be mom and her pals would come together, play some odd games (like smelling a chocolate-filled diaper—yes, that's a thing), and give gifts for the baby. But times are changing, and now it's not only acceptable, but downright cool for dads-to-be to get in on the action.

Who Plans This Shindig, Anyway? Traditionally, a close friend or family member (not from the immediate family) would have taken the reins. But these days, anyone can throw a baby shower. It's even okay for you and your partner to plan your own, if you so desire.

What's Your Role, Mr. Dad-to-Be? Aside from showing up and not embarrassing yourself too much, there are a few things you might be roped into:

1. **Games:** Even if the games sound a bit cheesy, get involved! There's nothing more heartwarming than watching a grown man try to guess the size of his pregnant partner's belly using a piece of string.
2. **Thank You's:** You'll get gifts. Hopefully a lot of them. Dive in and help with the thank you notes. It's all about teamwork!

Gender Reveal Revelry: A Pink or Blue Party?

Gender reveals have gone from simple cake-cutting affairs to elaborate events where things sometimes explode (seriously, keep it safe, folks).

These parties are often the first time friends and family, and sometimes even the expectant parents themselves, learn the baby's gender. They can range from the straightforward (like bursting a balloon to shower pink or blue confetti) to the more elaborate (such as setting off a modest fireworks display).

Who Plans This? It's common for a close friend or family member to plan the gender reveal, particularly if they're in on the secret of the baby's gender. However, it's also perfectly fine for the parents-to-be to take the reins and plan the event themselves.

What Do You Need to Do?

1. **Decide If You Want One:** This is a personal choice. Some folks love the excitement, while others prefer to find out the old-fashioned way!

2. **Safety First:** You don't want your gender reveal to end up on a "fails" compilation on the Internet.

3. **Enjoy the Moment:** This is a special time. No matter what color the confetti, cake, or smoke ends up being, the important thing is that your little one is celebrated and loved.

Navigating these social rituals might seem daunting, but remember, they're all about celebrating the upcoming arrival of your little one. Join in, have fun, and cherish these memories.

Mastering the Art of "Thank You": Graciously Accepting Gifts and Well Wishes

Gifts and well wishes are about to rain down on you like a sudden downpour in the summer, but not all gifts are going to be winners. You might end up with five copies of the same dad jokes book—and if you do, it's important to always remain gracious.

Let me share a light-hearted moment from my own journey. My aunt hand-knitted a sweater for our baby. The design was unique, to say the least. What made it truly special, though, wasn't the sweater itself, but the warm, proud smile she wore when she gave it to us. It reminded me that sometimes it's the thought and love behind a gift that truly matters, not just the gift itself.

The art of saying "thank you" is not just about being polite—it's about valuing the thought behind the gift. When someone hands you a present or sends a card, they're sharing a piece of their heart and saying they're happy for you.

Tips for Navigating the Gift Gauntlet:

1. **Smile, Even If It's Forced:** Some gifts will inevitably be a bit strange. Remember that it's the thought that counts, and smile, even if it's for a diaper genie that looks like it's from another dimension.

2. **Keep a List:** When the presents start piling up, it's easy to forget who gave you what. Jot it down quickly on your phone. This will help when you're sending out thank you cards or messages.

3. **Exchange and Regift Thoughtfully:** If you have duplicates or things you won't use, consider exchanging them or passing them on to someone who can use them. Just be careful not to regift to the original giver!

Invasion of the Relatives: Setting Boundaries and Maintaining Sanity

With a new baby on the way or newly arrived, it can sometimes feel like you've lit a beacon for all of your relatives. They mean well, but let's face it—sometimes you just want some space to breathe, bond with the baby, and catch up on some much-needed Zzz's.

I remember the time when two sets of aunts and uncles decided to visit our newborn—all on the same day! Let's just say it turned into a scene straight out of a sitcom, with me playing the lead role of a headless chicken.

Here's how to handle the incoming tide of well-meaning relatives:

1. **Communicate:** It might sound simple, but a quick heads-up about your wishes can save a lot of hassle. It's okay to tell folks that you'd appreciate a call before they drop by.

2. **Set Visit Times:** Instead of an open-door policy, consider having specific visiting hours. That way, you and your partner can still have some quiet time.

3. **It's Okay to Say "No":** If you're not up for visitors, that's okay. This is your time with your baby and partner. Don't feel pressured to entertain.

4. **Designate Helpers:** Got some relatives who are eager to be involved? Great! Ask them to help out—maybe with groceries, cooking, or even babysitting while you take a quick nap.

Safety is also an important consideration. With undeveloped immune systems, newborns are vulnerable to a wide variety of illnesses and infections. It's essential to:

- **Emphasize Hygiene:** Always insist on handwashing before anyone handles the baby. While face-kissing is affectionate, it should be avoided, especially in the early weeks. Common adult illnesses transferred through saliva can be more severe for babies. Additionally, the HSV-1 virus, responsible for cold sores, can cause complications in infants, even if the kisser doesn't show visible symptoms.

- **Discuss Vaccinations:** If you feel strongly about it, communicate your preference for visitors to have updated vaccinations, especially flu and Tdap. The CDC provides guidelines for vaccines recommended for family members and caregivers around newborns. Check it out here.

- **Set Clear Handling Rules:** Decide in advance who gets to hold the baby. Will it be adults only? Close family members? Making these choices pre-arrival ensures you and your partner present a united front.

Remember, boundaries are not barriers to family and friends. They're there to ensure everyone gets the best out of this special time. The key is communication, understanding, and lots of patience.

Handling Unsolicited Advice: Smile, Nod, and Run for the Diaper Bag

Imagine walking into your favorite coffee shop, the one where the barista knows not just your name, but also that you're about to become a dad. Without invitation, he hits you with the admonition, "You know, coffee is bad for pregnant women." Your eyebrow raises, a forced smile emerges, and you're left standing there, latte in hand, contemplating when exactly you asked for this piece of advice.

When you are about to become a parent, suddenly everyone has something to say about it. From old wives' tales to do's and don'ts that may or may not have a scientific basis, advice is hurled at you from every direction—family, friends, and yes, sometimes even baristas.

I recall a moment from my own impending fatherhood, when I was confidently informed by a stranger that allowing my pregnant wife to eat strawberries would surely result in a baby with a strawberry birthmark! I did my best not to snort my soda through my nose, and thanked them for their "wisdom."

When navigating this flood of unsolicited advice, the smile-and-nod technique becomes your best ally. The key isn't shutting down every piece of unwanted advice with a witty retort or a blunt rebuttal. Instead, it's about picking your battles and preserving your energy for where it's truly needed—supporting your partner and preparing for the arrival of your little one.

Every piece of unasked advice is like a little gift. You didn't ask for it, you don't necessarily want it, but you accept it graciously because it's the thought that counts. Who knows, among the pile of "Be sure to hang garlic above the crib to ward off evil spirits" (yes, that's a real piece of advice I received), there might be a genuine nugget of wisdom that you find helpful—or, at the very least, amusing.

Unsolicited Advice Survival Kit: Handling Well-Meaning but Overbearing Relatives

Nate, a new dad I met at a parenting class, shared a comical yet very relatable story. He was at a family gathering when his Aunt Patty, known for her unrequested guidance, approached him. Before she could launch into her latest spiel about how his newborn should sleep exclusively on sheepskin to "foster a connection to nature" (or something along those lines), he gently placed a hand on hers, looked deeply into her eyes, and said, "Patty, can I ask you something very important?" Aunt Patty, visibly touched and perhaps expecting a profound moment, nodded. Nate continued, "Do you think pineapples belong on pizza?"

What Nate brilliantly exhibited was a technique from the Unsolicited Advice Survival Kit: The Playful Deflect. By throwing a curveball question, he successfully sidetracked Aunt Patty into a harmless debate about pizza toppings, instead of having to listen to the benefits of sheepskin for the hundredth time.

Let's walk through the toolkit together, going over a number of other techniques that will help you gracefully navigate the sea of unsought counsel:

1. **The Genuine Appreciation:** Sometimes, a simple "Thank you for caring enough to share that with me" is sufficient. Acknowledge their intention, which is typically to be helpful, even if their advice is not.

2. **The Non-Committal Agree:** You'll perfect this with practice. It's the "Hmm, that's interesting!" or "I'll think about it!" strategy, which neither agrees nor disagrees with the advice provided.

3. **The Subject Change:** Swiftly transition the conversation to a different topic. If Uncle Bob is insistent on telling you the best diaper brand, divert by discussing his famous BBQ ribs recipe instead.

4. **The Curious Questioner:** If Aunt Mary is certain that a specific lullaby will ensure your child's acceptance into Harvard, ask her to tell you more about how lullabies impacted her own kids. This isn't about accepting advice, but steering the narrative into storytelling mode, which most relatives adore.

5. **The Firm Boundary:** If playful and gentle tactics aren't doing the trick, it's essential to set boundaries. A heartfelt "I value your experience and advice, but we've decided to take a different approach with our baby" may be necessary to firmly convey your stance.

6. **The Partner Pivot:** Have a code with your partner for when you need a "rescue." A simple "Honey, could you help me with this?" can grant you a much-needed exit from an advice-heavy conversation.

7. **The Humor Card:** Sometimes, responding with a light-hearted joke or sharing a funny baby related meme can keep things friendly and diffuse the advice onslaught. Have a couple handy (or saved in your phone's folder/album) for a quick diversion.

Remember that these tools aren't just for deflecting advice, but also for preserving relationships and ensuring interactions remain harmonious—even when besieged with an endless barrage of parenting dos and don'ts.

One essential note: Advice, especially from older relatives, will often be outdated. Parenting has evolved immensely in recent decades. For instance, it was once common practice to lay babies on their stomachs for sleep, but today, the American Academy of Pediatrics (AAP) recommends babies sleep on their backs to reduce the risk of SIDS. Likewise, in past generations, many parents were advised to wait around a year to introduce solid food. However, the current guidance from the AAP is to start complementary foods at around six months, while also noting that some babies might be ready by as early as four months. Always consult with a pediatrician to determine the best approach for your child.

It is important to recognize that much of the advice you receive comes from a place of love and genuine concern, based on practices from when and where the advice-giver raised their children. However, with advancements in research and understanding, many guidelines have changed. It's crucial to stay informed and trust contemporary, research-backed guidelines, while also acknowledging the intent behind the older advice you receive.

From a Woman's Perspective: Actionable, Practical Steps to Take

Reflecting on our experience with pregnancy announcements, baby showers, and the cascade of advice, I realize there were nuances I wish my husband had instinctively understood. These insights are not just personal recollections, but key lessons for every dad-to-be. Understanding and acting on these will empower you to support your partner effectively through the bustling social aspects of pregnancy.

Collaborative Approach to Announcements: Your partner might feel a mix of excitement and anxiety when sharing the pregnancy news. It's crucial that the announcement reflects both of your styles and preferences.

- **Action Steps:** Have a conversation about how you both would like to announce the pregnancy. Whether it's a creative reveal or an intimate family gathering, ensure it's a joint decision that celebrates your unique journey into parenthood.

Involvement in Baby Shower Planning: Baby showers can sometimes be overwhelming, particularly when you factor in traditions and expectations. Your partner might appreciate transforming it into a celebration that feels authentic to both of you.

- **Action Steps:** Actively participate in planning the baby shower. Your involvement, from contributing ideas to helping with organization, can turn it into a special event that resonates with both of you.

Handling Unsolicited Advice Together: Throughout the pregnancy, your partner will likely receive a lot of advice, both welcome and unsolicited. She might hope for your support in navigating these suggestions.

- **Action Steps:** Listen politely to advice, but later discuss with your partner which suggestions align with your parenting philosophy. Your united front in this regard will strengthen your shared vision for parenting.

Managing Visits from Relatives and Friends: After the birth, your partner might find herself balancing the excitement of friends and family with the need for privacy.

- **Action Steps:** Help set visiting boundaries that work for both of you. Encourage visitors to call ahead or schedule their visits, ensuring you both have the space you need during this significant transition.

Staying Centered Amid Celebrations: In the midst of baby showers and gender reveals, it's important to remain focused on what truly matters—your growing family.

- **Action Steps:** Amid the festivities, take time to connect with your partner. Discuss your feelings about the pregnancy and the future, keeping the foundation of your relationship strong.

For all dads-to-be, it's important to remember that these social occasions are more than just events; they're opportunities to deepen your relationship and actively participate in the pregnancy journey.

Your partner values your empathy, understanding, and involvement in making this time a shared and joyful experience. This phase is not only about celebrating, but also nurturing the bond you have and preparing for your new family role.

Key Takeaways

This chapter equips you for the unique challenges and joys of preparing for your baby's arrival, from managing announcements and baby showers to handling family dynamics and unsolicited advice. Embrace these experiences with grace, humor, and joy.

- **Creativity in Announcements:** Embrace unique and personal ways to announce your pregnancy, whether through a fun T-shirt, a custom puzzle, a creative movie poster, or a simple yet heartfelt social media post. The method you choose should reflect your personality and relationship.

- **Navigating Baby Registries:** Approach baby registries with a focus on essentials. Consult experienced parents for practical advice on must-have items, and remember it's okay to make changes based on your baby's unique needs.

- **Participating in Baby Showers:** Engage actively in baby showers, embracing games and helping with thank you notes. The involvement signifies your commitment to the parenting journey and appreciation for the support network.

- **Handling Gender Reveals:** Make the gender reveal a personal choice, prioritizing safety and enjoyment. Whether it's a simple balloon pop or a more elaborate event, the focus should be on celebrating the baby.

- **Gracious Acceptance of Gifts:** No matter the nature of the gifts received, showing gratitude is key. Remember that each gift represents someone's care and excitement for your new family.

- **Managing Relative Invasions:** Set boundaries with visiting relatives, emphasizing hygiene and safety, especially for the newborn. Utilize communication and planning to manage visits and maintain your family's comfort.

- **Dealing with Unsolicited Advice:** Develop strategies to gracefully handle unsolicited advice, using tactics like appreciation, subject change, humor, and firm boundaries. Remember, the advice often comes from a place of love and concern.

- **Staying Informed and Updated:** Recognize the evolution in parenting practices and rely on current, research-backed guidelines for child-rearing, while appreciating the intent behind older, possibly outdated advice.

Chapter Five

COMFORT FOR MOM: TOOLS AND TIPS FOR A SMOOTH PREGNANCY

"Knowledge is the key to a comfortable pregnancy."
— *Dr. Jane Smith*

Pregnancy involves more than just preparing for the baby's arrival. It can be tough for expectant mothers, who often deal with late-night cravings, back pain, and emotional ups and downs. Our job as men is to support and care for them throughout these nine months, making sure they're as comfortable and stress-free as possible.

We'll dig into the simple stuff, like making sure her pillows are just the right amount of fluffy, as well as the slightly trickier stuff, like figuring out which of those gadgets at the store will make her (and your) life a smidge easier.

In this chapter, we're tackling the practical, essential, and downright fun ways to ensure you're both basking in as much joy and comfort as possible.

Pillow Talk: Creating a Sleep-Friendly Environment for Mom

When it comes to pregnancy, nighttime can have its fair share of challenges. This time is all about ensuring comfort and attending to unexpected desires, from setting up the perfect sleep environment to going on sudden snack adventures.

As pregnancy progresses, particularly into the second trimester, your typical cushions will likely no longer be adequate. Dave spent considerable time researching the perfect pregnancy pillow for his partner, exploring options like C-shaped, U-shaped, and others, to ensure her comfort during the pregnancy. These specialty pillows, often generously sized, offer the right support for the belly, back, and knees, helping facilitate a peaceful night's rest.

But sleep prep wasn't Dave's only duty. As the months passed, late-night snack runs became increasingly important. Whether it was a 3:00 AM hankering for grilled cheese or a quirky combo of pickles and peanut butter, these nocturnal escapades, although tiring, deepened the couple's connection. Each satisfied craving was a clear message: "No matter the hour or request, I'm here."

Creating the optimal sleep environment requires attention to a wide variety of details. For example, a good mattress can make a world of difference. If yours isn't in the best shape, consider getting a memory foam topper. It adds an extra layer of cushioning, which is beneficial for those undergoing pregnancy's physical changes.

Ambiance is also important. With pregnancy often comes increased body heat, which makes cool, breathable sheets a necessity. Fabrics like bamboo or others that wick away moisture keep things comfortable. For those disturbed by external noises, a white noise machine might be a worthwhile investment, ensuring uninterrupted sleep for both of you.

As you accompany your partner through the ups and downs of pregnancy, realize that every little effort counts. By creating a comfortable sleep setting and staying responsive to her ever-evolving needs, you're strengthening your bond and forging a connection that will continue to grow once your baby arrives. Enjoy these moments, from setting up cushions to midnight snack runs—they're memories in the making.

The Power of Touch: Massage Techniques for Pregnancy Bliss

Your partner's body is serving as a cushy, cozy home for your future offspring. Imagine carrying around a progressively heavy, awkwardly shaped bag for several months. Backaches, sore shoulders, and stiff necks are a daily occurrence, so do what you can to help alleviate the discomfort.

You might be thinking, "But I don't know the first thing about giving a massage!" Fear not! It's not about performing professional-level massages—it's about providing comfort, showing empathy, and being present. Your hands are about to become the best part of your partner's day.

Start with the shoulders, a common place where tension resides. Gentle circular motions with your thumbs, working your way from the neck outward to the tips of the shoulders, can ease the tension momentarily. Be attentive. If she winces or tenses up, lighten your touch. If she lets out an "Ahhh," you're probably on the right path.

The lower back is a region that supports the entire pregnancy operation. Cupping your hands on either side of the spine and executing delicate, upwards sweeps towards the mid-back can work wonders. It's crucial not to press down. Think of your hands as fluffy clouds, gently rolling along the landscape of her back.

Hands and feet also enjoy a little pampering—and since swollen feet are inevitable during pregnancy, some gentle foot rubs might just elevate you to "partner of the year" status. Gentle rotations at the ankles, light pulls at the toes, and soft kneading on the soles can provide a blissful reprieve from the daily pains of pregnancy.

There are also areas and pressure points to avoid during pregnancy. Sticking to light, gentle massages and avoiding deep-tissue techniques is your safest bet. The aim is not to resolve muscle issues, but to provide a loving touch, comfort, and a momentary break from the physical demands of carrying a growing human.

Supporting your partner during pregnancy is about more than just providing physical relief. It's also about emotional connection—about being there and sharing this unique, amazing, and occasionally back-aching journey together. Your gentle touch conveys love, appreciation, and shared anticipation for the little bundle that will soon turn your duo into a trio.

The Zen Zone: Stress-Relieving Activities for Mom's Serenity

If you've followed the hands-on advice from the last section, you're now semi-proficient in kneading away physical tension. But what about the emotional and mental tension that pregnancy brings to Mom?

A pregnant friend of mine named Sam was frantically preparing for a new chapter of life. Her partner, Dan, could see her stress levels rising. He realized that providing a relaxing refuge was crucial, not just for Sam, but for their tiny human-to-be, as well.

Dan rolled up his sleeves and dove into crafting the "Zen Zone." This was a tranquil space where stress was forbidden, where serene vibes floated around, and where Sam could escape from the chaotic whirlwind of the external world.

Your first tool in establishing a zen paradise of your own is empathy. Understanding the emotional roller coaster your partner is riding can pave the way for a smoother journey together. Every good amusement park has a chill-out zone, and your job is to create one for her.

Create a cozy nook in the house where the pillows are plumper than a Michelin-star soufflé, the light is soft and mellow, and the outside world stays outside. Populate it with things that bring her joy. Maybe it's that hilariously bad movie she loves, a playlist that puts her in a good mood, or a scent that soothes her stress.

Get creative and establish rituals for the "Zen Zone." These could include a daily unwinding yoga session together, a "no phone zone" where you just talk (or don't talk) and simply revel in each other's calm company, or an arts and crafts hour (adult coloring books can be astonishingly therapeutic).

You might be thinking, "But, I can barely manage my own stress, how can I curate serenity for two?" Your attempts, however imperfect, will mean the world. You don't have to completely eliminate stress—you just have to provide a haven from it, even if it's only temporary.

This "Zen Zone" will not only be a fortress of tranquility for Mom, but also a space where you both can bond, grow, and prepare for the wonderful chaos about to grace your lives. Embark on this journey with a compassionate heart and creative spirit, and build something special for your growing family.

Surviving Swollen Feet and Backaches: Remedies and Reliefs

During pregnancy, your partner may experience physical discomforts like swollen feet and backaches. While you can't directly experience these discomforts yourself, there are practical and supportive ways you can help alleviate them:

1. **Provide Foot Relief:** Swollen feet can be a common issue. Consider getting comfortable, supportive slippers or arranging a relaxing foot soak. Offering to gently massage her feet with cooling lotions or gels can also provide relief.

2. **Backache Solutions:** Back pain is another frequent discomfort. Applying heat or cold packs can offer some relief. If you're unsure about massage techniques, consider booking a professional prenatal massage for her.

Tim and Sally were working hard to navigate the ever-changing terrain of pregnancy together. Having read ahead, Tim turned their living room into a mini-oasis for Sally's swollen extremities. Pillows, a foot spa, and her favorite snacks were all within arm's reach. Tim didn't have a degree in reflexology or chiropractic expertise, but his actions whispered, "I'm here, I'm with you, and your comfort matters to me."

All of the little things add up. You're not expected to have all the answers or solutions, but your genuine care, attention, and creative attempts at bringing comfort make you an MVP in this journey.

Pro Tip: Invest in practical tools that can alleviate some of the common discomforts of pregnancy. Consider getting her belly support bands to help distribute the baby's weight more evenly, compression socks to mitigate swelling, and knee supports for added stability. While these may not be the most glamorous gifts, they will be met with gratitude when the physical challenges of pregnancy rear their ugly heads.

Nourishing Mom and Baby: Easy and Nutritious Meal Ideas

Cooking up a storm in the kitchen might seem daunting, but nutritious, simple meals to nourish both Mom and Baby are totally doable. With pregnancy, the nutritional needs of your partner and the growing baby increase, and it's largely up to you to meet them.

Joe thought he had maxed out his cooking skills with instant noodles, but when his partner Lisa's cravings began to resemble a festive food fair, he realized it was time to diversify. With love as his compass and a handy slow cooker by his side, he ventured into the land of easy, nutritious meals. Lentils, colorful veggies, and a pinch of seasoning turned into a wholesome stew by sunset. No chef credentials needed!

Your mealtime mantra is lean proteins, whole grains, an array of veggies, and the occasional treat (dark chocolate!). If mac 'n' cheese is her current love, mix in some pureed veggies for a secret nutrient boost.

It's important to remember that some foods are off the table during pregnancy. These include certain fish that are high in mercury (like shark and swordfish), raw or undercooked seafood, unpasteurized dairy products, and deli meats (unless they're fully reheated).

Hydration is also important! Pregnant women need more water than usual. The Institute of Medicine recommends about 10 cups (2.3 liters) daily during pregnancy. Water aids in forming the placenta, which transports nutrients to the baby. It also helps in the production of amniotic fluid and supports digestion, which can help ease constipation, a common pregnancy symptom.

Your job is to ensure a balanced, joyful food journey. If a scoop of ice cream lights up her eyes, embrace it! Be the comforting partner full of warmth, understanding, and a surprise snack when she needs it most.

Dad's Toolbox: Pregnancy Comfort Essentials: Stuff That Make a Difference

As you progress through the later stages of pregnancy with your partner, you'll find yourself dealing with some of the less glamorous aspects of expectancy. An expanding belly, swelling feet, and backaches can all become common. As a supportive partner, it's essential to know how you can help alleviate her discomfort. In this section, we'll provide you with a guide to the essential items and strategies that can genuinely ease the challenges of these later stages of pregnancy.

1. The Marvelous Pregnancy Pillow: Every pregnant woman's dream is a good night's sleep—and this pillow is like a fluffy cloud sent from the heavens. Designed to offer support to her growing belly and alleviate back pain, it's the closest thing to a magic wand you'll find. As a bonus, once the baby's out, you can totally borrow it for those post-binge-watching nap sessions.

2. Massage Gadgets: You don't need to be a certified masseuse to offer relief. Devices like hand-held massagers or even simple massage rollers can work wonders. If your partner looks at you with the same admiration she has for a large pizza, you're doing it right.

3. Foot Spa: No, not a fancy day-out, but a nifty little device you can set up at home. Your partner's feet are working overtime, carrying an extra load. A warm foot spa session while you both binge on your favorite show is her idea of a perfect night.

4. Cooling Packs: These handy packs can be lifesavers for swollen ankles, tender breasts or aching backs. They're like those cool packs you use for sprains, but target pregnancy aches and pains instead.

5. Belly Creams and Oils: With the skin stretching, itching and dryness can be real issues. A good belly cream or oil can offer relief. If you really want to score brownie points, offer to apply it for her. It's bonding time, plus it prevents stretch marks.

6. Compression Socks: They're not the fanciest fashion statement, but they can do wonders for swollen feet and ankles.

Remember, while these tools can provide physical comfort, your emotional support, patience, and understanding are the real winners. Every time you hand over that massager or set up the foot spa, it's not just about the gadget, but also the love and care behind it.

 # From a Woman's Perspective: Actionable, Practical Steps to Take

During our pregnancy journey, I realized there were aspects I wished my husband had been more aware of. This includes understanding the comfort needed for a changing body and providing emotional support as the due date approaches.

Understanding the Pillow Fortress: Your partner's sleep comfort is crucial, and her side of the bed is now a fortress of pillows. Each one is strategically placed for support, but this setup can make getting in and out of bed a bit of a challenge, especially during those frequent nighttime bathroom visits.

- **Action Steps:** Become an adept co-navigator of her pillow fortress. Assist with getting in and out of bed, and install soft night lights to guide the path to the bathroom at night.

Anticipating Daily Challenges: Pregnancy brings new challenges in mobility and flexibility. Simple tasks like bending over or clipping toenails can become unexpectedly difficult for her. Remember, the bigger her belly gets, the harder it is for her to move around, so she needs your help!

- **Action Steps:** Be observant and proactive. Take over tasks that are becoming difficult for your partner, such as loading the dishwasher, taking care of laundry, etc. Any tasks that require bending or lifting heavy things should be moved to your to-do list.

Proactive Relief for Aches and Pains: As her body changes and adapts to pregnancy, she may experience various discomforts, from a sore back to general aches and pains. The list of discomforts is too long to list here. Basically, it starts to feel like everything that can hurt, actually does. The knees, feet, back, hips, toes...everything hurts. It's also important to note that she may have to avoid certain pain relief medications that aren't suitable for pregnant women, so that's where you step in.

- **Action Steps:** When you notice signs of discomfort, offer back rubs or a warm bath with bubbles and epsom salt. Foot rubs are great for tired and swollen feet that feel like they're on fire. These gestures are deeply appreciated and can significantly ease physical discomfort.

Simplifying Meals Thoughtfully: Nutritional needs and meal preparation can become more complex during pregnancy. Simple, healthy meals are essential for both her well-being and time management.

- **Action Steps:** Learn to prepare nutritious, straightforward meals that can become your new go-to dishes. Consider making meals in bulk for easy reheating, as this will reduce daily cooking stress.

Your support and understanding during this journey are invaluable. You and your partner are building a foundation of love and shared joy as you prepare for your new arrival. Let these insights guide you in this remarkable journey together.

Key Takeaways

Navigating the challenges of pregnancy with your partner involves a mix of practical support and emotional understanding. Here are four key takeaways to ensure you're doing your part as a supportive partner:

1. **Comfort Gear:** Prepare pregnancy pillows and massage tools to alleviate physical discomfort.
2. **Listen More:** Provide a supportive presence rather than quick-fix solutions.
3. **Be Proactive:** Stay ahead of needs and schedules to lighten her mental load.
4. **Personal Respect:** Honor her personal space and support her interests beyond the pregnancy.

The perfect blend of practical support and heartfelt understanding makes all the difference during the transformative months of pregnancy, creating a strong foundation for your shared journey into parenthood.

Chapter Six

THE BIG DAY: LABOR, DELIVERY, AND LIFE-CHANGING MOMENTS

"Being a great father is like shaving. No matter how good you shaved today, you have to do it again tomorrow."

— *Reed Markham*

John was a future dad whose life was punctuated with moments of calm and routine. Suddenly, his world imploded with a two-word announcement: "It's time!" His heart beat uncontrollably; his eyes were wide and glazed with a mixture of joy and disbelief.

Through the cascade of emotions, John found a steady current of resolve. There was no turning back now-—not that he'd want to. This crazy, beautiful day was the gateway to a new chapter.

With the birth of your child, the life you have known is inexorably changed—it is richened with an endless progression of vivid, exhilarating experiences that are uniquely yours. It's here, in these moments of anticipation, exhilaration, and sometimes fear, that you'll embark on the most profound adventure of all.

Spotting the Telltale Signs of Labor

Entering the crucial stages of labor and delivery, expectant fathers often grapple with a cascade of emotions, anticipation, and anxiety. Fortunately, we will be going over a number of clear signs of labor, ensuring you're equipped with all of the knowledge you need.

Water Breaking: Despite the name, this won't always be a deluge. Sometimes, it's just a subtle leak. But when your partner announces it's time, it's essential that you take her word for it.

Contractions: Not to be confused with the sporadic Braxton Hicks, authentic contractions have a systematic pattern and intensify steadily.

Back Pain: Beyond the typical ache from toting extra weight, a relentless, dull pain that refuses to ease may indicate it's the real deal.

Nesting Instinct Kicks into High Gear: Although we've discussed nesting previously, when it suddenly amplifies, it might be a subtle hint that your partner's body is gearing up.

Losing the Mucus Plug: As uninviting as it sounds, this is a natural signal declaring, "Buckle up, Dad, it's almost time."

While these signs can offer guidance, labor doesn't necessarily stick to a set script. It may throw unexpected scenarios your way, and in those instances, your partner needs you to be calm, composed, and comforting. Keep the car ready, the hospital bag packed, and a comforting playlist prepped to lighten the mood en route to the hospital.

At times, signs of labor may be misleading. They might progress much more slowly than expected, or they might progress rapidly. In any situation, maintaining open communication with the health care provider is vital to navigate the process smoothly and safely. Your role is to be the unwavering support system, ensuring everything is on track and that morale remains high as you welcome a new member into your family.

Your partner may not recall the journey to the hospital or the color of the delivery room walls, but she will remember how you made her feel—acknowledged, cherished, and supported.

Supporting Mom Through Contractions and Pain Relief Options

Labor has officially kicked off, and the contractions are starting to flow. It's a bit like an out-of-body experience, watching someone you adore go through such a profoundly intense moment. Even though you aren't directly involved, you can still find small, meaningful ways to mitigate the discomfort and assure her she's not alone in this journey.

I remember being taken aback by how the woman I loved was wrestling with so much pain, trying to ride through each contraction with as much poise as she could muster. But there was also an unspoken agreement between us that I, too, was part of this moment, trying to shoulder some of the emotional burden, even if the physical one was hers alone to bear.

In the midst of contractions, touch becomes a language of its own. Light back rubs, gentle strokes of her arm, squeezing hips, or simply holding her hand can convey a reassurance that words often fall short of providing.

She'll often guide you on how to help her best. Remain attentive and read her cues, even when she might not be able to articulate them. Is she squeezing your hand tighter? Is she leaning into your touch or away from it?

Also consider your verbal support. Gentle words of encouragement can work wonders, but it is important to gauge her response. Some moms find solace in soothing words, while others might prefer quiet. It's a balancing act of empathy, encouragement, and understanding.

When it comes to pain relief, epidurals, and alternative methods like using a birthing ball or water birth, there are a lot of choices, and your role is to help your partner navigate them. Maybe she had a birth plan, penned meticulously months before, outlining her wish to go all-natural—but in the throes of labor, she's reconsidering. Help facilitate communication with the medical team, ensuring her wishes are heard and respected, even if they change mid-process.

Whichever route she decides to take with pain management, your emotional and physical support are of the utmost importance. Whether she chooses an epidural, opts for breathing techniques, or pursues a completely different mode of pain management, stay flexible, supportive, and, most of all, present.

And while you're at it, don't forget to breathe yourself. You might not be the one in physical pain, but the emotional toll can sneak up on you. Steal a few moments for a quick breath, a sip of coffee, or a chat with a family member or friend. You're riding your own wave of emotions, and maintaining your well-being is crucial so that you can truly be there for her and the little one about to make an entrance into your world.

A Listening Ear and Being Proactive

When the contractions hit, it's likely that communication from your partner will be minimal—or, in some instances, slightly incoherent. Listen intently. Sometimes, a squeeze of your hand might be a call for reassurance; a knitted brow might signal discomfort that needs alleviating; and a shudder might be a plea for a soothing word or two. It's all about deciphering those non-verbal cues and acting accordingly, ensuring she feels heard, seen, and supported.

- **Sweat:** See it glistening on her forehead? Gently dab it away.
- **Breathe:** In sync with her. Counting breaths can guide her through contractions.
- **Hot:** Reach for a damp cloth and a handheld fan.
- **Water:** She's likely parched. A sip can make a difference.

- **Cold:** Fetch that warm blanket.
- **Hips:** Brace and provide pressure on her hips during the next contraction.

Being attentive to these cues can provide immeasurable comfort during the demanding hours of labor.

Designate a Support Person and Decide Who Else Will Be in the Delivery Room

The birth of a child is a pivotal and emotional event, and the delivery room is the center of this experience. It's a place where intense emotions and physical challenges converge. While the focus is primarily on the mother and the baby, there can also be space for an additional support person. This individual can provide extra support alongside the father, helping to create a more comforting and reassuring environment during labor and delivery.

The additional support person isn't just there for the partner in labor, but also for the dad-to-be. I remember when my partner was in labor. The atmosphere was thick with anticipation, and there was a subtle churn of anxiety in my stomach. But our doula, a calm, reassuring presence, gently squeezed my shoulder, offering silent strength and understanding.

Deciding Who to Let In

Choosing who gets to be present in the delivery room isn't always a walk in the park. It's a delicate decision, balancing the comfort and wishes of the laboring partner with the emotional support needs of the dad-to-be. It could be a close friend, a relative, or a professional, like a doula.

Jim and his partner chose her sister—an unflappable woman who had sailed through two labors of her own. She wasn't just a comforting presence for the mom-to-be, but also a pragmatic, empathetic support for Jim, guiding him gently through every crest and trough of the labor experience.

Cultivating the Ideal Support Dynamic

It's important to communicate transparently and set boundaries with your chosen support person. The more you decide ahead of time, the more smoothly things will go. What role will they play? How can they best support both of you? What are your partner's comfort level and privacy needs during labor?

In our case, the numerous candid conversations we had with our doula before D-Day were invaluable. They enabled her to straddle the delicate line between being supportively present and respectfully distant during the intensely personal moments of labor and birth.

Their Role

In the throes of labor, a support person transforms into a multifaceted support pillar. They may whisper words of encouragement, share the emotional load with the dad, provide physical support, or simply hold space for both parents to experience the unfolding miracle in their own unique way.

Our doula seamlessly transitioned from offering gentle back rubs to my partner to sharing a knowing, supportive glance with me and quietly ensuring that our birth plan was being respected and followed by the medical team.

Picture Perfect: Capturing Precious Moments in the Delivery Room

During childbirth, emotions can be intense. It's often the small, unscripted moments that capture the essence of the experience. While it's challenging to put the feeling of seeing your child for the first time into words, photographs can capture these priceless moments. These images become cherished memories, encapsulating the raw emotions and joy of birth.

I recall when my best friend, Jake, became a dad. In the midst of all the anticipation and nerves, he managed to capture his daughter's very first yawn. It wasn't the most polished photo—no professional lighting or staged backdrop—but it had heart, sincerity, and a sense of realness that no studio portrait could match.

Consider having your support person double as the photographer and videographer, allowing you to concentrate fully on your partner. And if you decide to be the one to take photos, make sure you have your gear and technique dialed in before D-Day.

Know Your Gear

Whether you're using your smartphone or a professional camera, understanding its basic functions is vital. Familiarize yourself with quick access buttons, focusing mechanisms, and flash settings. You don't want to be fumbling around while your partner is having contractions.

Respect the Moment

Remember, you're there primarily to support your partner. Photographs are secondary. Never let the process of capturing memories interfere with being present and assisting your partner. It's best to have another person take care of the photos, so you can focus.

Consider Hiring a Professional

If you want to ensure high-quality shots without the stress of doing it yourself, consider hiring a birth photographer. They're trained to work in low-light conditions and are adept at capturing intimate moments without intruding.

Check Hospital Policies

Before bringing out your camera or smartphone, ensure you're not violating hospital or birthing center regulations. Not everyone is comfortable being photographed, especially in such vulnerable moments. Always check with your partner and the medical team before clicking away.

Backup and Storage

Once you've captured those special moments, ensure they're safe. Transfer them to cloud storage or an external drive as soon as possible. It would be heartbreaking to lose irreplaceable memories due to a tech glitch or mishap.

When you look back years later, these photographs will be a reminder of the emotions you felt on that monumental day. Like Jake, who often revisits that candid shot of his daughter's first yawn, you too will have a tangible memory of a day that changed your life forever. Just remember, while photos are great keepsakes, nothing beats living in the moment and cherishing it firsthand.

Dad's Delivery Room Toolbox

As we approach the day of delivery, it's crucial to be prepared for the unpredictable nature of the delivery room. It's a place where calm can quickly turn to urgency, and your role as a supportive partner is key. To help you navigate this crucial setting effectively, let's explore the Delivery Room Toolbox. This collection of essentials and knowledge will equip you to provide the best possible support to your partner, ensuring you're both ready for the momentous experience ahead.

1. The Playlist of Positivity: Music is a potent mood elevator. Curate a playlist that combines both your partner's favorite tunes and a selection of songs that have been meaningful in your relationship. Not only will it provide a familiar and comforting background score, but it might also serve as a light distraction and spirit-lifter in the midst of contractions.

2. The Snack Pack Surprise: Yes, snacks were discussed previously, but we can't ever get enough! In addition to the regular snacks, surprise your partner with a rare treat she's been missing or a nostalgic snack that harkens back to a sweet memory, providing a brief escape and a smile amid the intensity of labor.

3. Coded Communication: Establish a set of secret, non-verbal signals between you and your partner. This covert communication method can serve to silently convey love, encouragement, or check-ins without needing to interrupt her focus during labor.

4. The Comfort Capsule: Prepare a small bag containing items like a comforting scent, a piece of soft fabric, or a personal item of yours. In moments of intensity, your partner can find solace in these tangible tokens that not only comfort her senses, but also serve as a physical connection to you when medical staff might need to keep you at a distance.

5. Memory Maker: Rather than just snapping photos, keep a tiny notebook where you can jot down feelings, observations, and notable moments during the labor and delivery process. Later, this can be transformed into a beautiful letter or story for your child, illustrating the awe and love present at their arrival into the world.

These thoughtfully prepared elements won't just offer tangible support and comfort to your partner, but also weave a gentle thread of shared experiences and secret smiles into the monumental occasion of your child's birth. It's not merely about surviving the delivery room, but also actively contributing to the atmosphere, supporting your partner, and creating a cocoon of shared love and support around both of you as you welcome your new arrival.

Staying Calm and Collected: Dad's Guide to Keeping Mom Comfortable During Labor

I recall observing my friend Tom during his wife's labor. From a distance, he appeared to be the epitome of calm, firmly holding his wife's hand. However, upon closer inspection, a different story unfolded. His hands subtly trembled, betraying his inner nerves. Despite this, his voice remained steady, his words were full of encouragement, and his focus on supporting his wife never wavered.

Your presence during labor, both physically and emotionally, is a pillar your partner will lean on. While Tom will admit he was a mess on the inside, externally, he was a haven of tranquility for his wife.

Let's discuss some simple yet profound ways that you, like Tom, can be the rock your partner needs during labor.

Educate Yourself

Understand the stages of labor, the possible scenarios, and the different medical interventions. This knowledge will make the process less intimidating and allow you to offer effective support and advocacy for your partner when she may not be able to do so herself.

Practice Breathing Together

Join your partner in prenatal classes and practice breathing exercises. Your ability to guide her through those techniques during labor will not only aid her, but also provide a subtle distraction from the pain.

Pack Wisely

Ensure you have a well-packed bag for the hospital. Include snacks, a change of clothes, essential toiletries, and anything your partner might find comforting, like a favorite pillow or preferred lip balm.

Provide Physical Comfort

Rubbing her back, holding her hand, or simply placing a cool cloth on her forehead can be immensely comforting. It's the little acts of kindness that convey your love and support, even without the need for words.

Encourage and Affirm

Your words of encouragement can be a well of strength for her to draw from. Gentle affirmations and validations like "You're doing great" or "I'm here for you" can mean the world in those intense moments.

Be Her Advocate

Understand her birth plan and be her voice when she may not be in a position to communicate her own wishes. Ensure that her preferences are respected to the greatest extent possible.

Prepare for Post-Birth

Once the baby arrives, your partner will be exhausted. Ensure you are ready to assist with diaper changes, swaddling, and handling the baby so she can rest.

Mind Your Own Well-Being

While your primary focus will be on your partner, do not neglect yourself entirely. A quick walk, a few deep breaths, or a brief chat with a family member can replenish your energy and keep you centered.

Be Prepared for Possible Complications: Know the Vocabulary

In my first moments as a new dad, I can remember the brief shock that ran through me when the doctor mentioned the term "meconium aspiration." My wife, Flora, and I thought we were well-prepared, but in that moment, I wished I had invested a bit more time in understanding some of the medical jargon related to childbirth complications.

Complications during labor can be nerve-wracking, especially when you're inundated with medical terminology that sounds intimidating. Let's decode a few of the more common terms.

Meconium Aspiration

This term may sound alien, but it merely refers to a situation where the baby has passed meconium (first feces) into the amniotic fluid during labor, and may inhale it into their lungs. It can pose risks, but health care professionals are adept at managing this common occurrence.

Preeclampsia

The moment I learned about preeclampsia from a friend's experience, it was easy to let the fear creep in. This is a condition characterized by high blood pressure in your pregnant partner, and it can have serious consequences if not managed properly. Knowledge about it can pave the way for constructive conversations with health care providers.

Breech Position

When a baby decides to make an entrance buttocks or feet first, that's called a breech position. This posture can make vaginal birth challenging, and sometimes leads doctors to suggest a C-section for safer delivery.

Umbilical Cord Prolapse

A situation that requires swift action, umbilical cord prolapse happens when the umbilical cord slips through the cervix before the baby, which could potentially compress it during delivery. It's vital to remain calm and trust the health care team, who are trained to handle this.

C-Section (Cesarean Section)

A C-section is a surgical procedure used to deliver the baby through incisions in the abdomen and uterus, often recommended when vaginal delivery might pose risks to the mother or baby.

Epidural

An epidural is a form of anesthesia used to numb pain, most commonly utilized during labor. Understanding its role and effects will help you support your partner in making an informed choice about pain management.

In the hustle and chaos that can arise during labor, your ability to understand these terms and communicate effectively with the medical team is crucial. When I witnessed Flora's C-section due to our baby being in a breech position, having clarity about these terms made the situation significantly less stressful. It allowed me to stay composed and be the supportive partner Flora needed, holding her hand and whispering assurances, knowing our capable team had things under control.

Witnessing Your Baby's First Breath—and Possibly Shedding a Tear (No Judgment!)

In the crisp and somewhat antiseptic air of the delivery room, I witnessed something that was paradoxically so routine yet miraculous at the same time—my baby's first breath. There, in a room filled with a bizarre mixture of calm professionalism and heightened anticipation, I saw my daughter take in the world in a gust of a breath—and then, with vigor, announce her arrival with a robust cry.

The tears caught me by surprise. Not Flora's—mine.

For many, the sight of their newborn's first breath and delicate cry is intensely personal and hugely powerful. To all dads-to-be reading this, no matter how composed you think you'll be, the emotionality of the moment can get you. The joy, the relief, the love—it can all come out at once

And that's perfectly okay.

My friend Jake is a burly man who normally wouldn't flinch, even in the most anxiety-ridden situations. He shared his experience with me, and perhaps it will resonate with you, too. While he stood there, mouth slightly agape, watching his son take his first breath, memories of the challenges, the late-night snack runs, and the sound of his pregnant wife's soft snores all dissolved into nothingness in the face of this new little being. A single tear slid down his cheek, an emotional testament to the miracle he'd just witnessed.

Tears are not a symbol of weakness. Your tears are a testament to your strength, your love, and the incredible journey you've just embarked upon. This is the first moment in a lifetime of moments that you'll experience as a dad.

As you wipe those tears away, know that they are not merely a product of the overwhelming emotions swirling inside you. They are also a symbol of the commitment, the love, and the myriad experiences that await you on this new path of fatherhood.

As I held Flora's trembling hand, both of our eyes fixated on the tiny being that was now part of our world, I realized that the tear that had involuntarily escaped me was not just out of joy or relief. It was a silent vow that whispered of protection, love, and a future where this tiny, breath-taking miracle would be cherished and loved unconditionally.

Prepare to be bowled over by love, new dads. When you lock eyes with your tiny human for the first time, it's a feeling unlike any other, an experience that is indescribably profound. It is a moment where all the complexity of the universe contracts into a single point of absolute simplicity.

The Golden Hour: Skin-to-Skin Contact and Bonding

Your first experience with your new baby is the "golden hour." It's that magical time right after birth when you have the opportunity to establish a connection that will form the bedrock of your relationship with the newest addition to your family.

This moment is crucial. Research indicates that immediate skin-to-skin contact between the newborn and parents (including fathers) significantly benefits the baby. Physical contact is not merely a warm embrace, but also a mechanism that helps regulate the baby's temperature and heart rate, and even aids in establishing breastfeeding for the mother (Crenshaw, 2014).

When your newborn is placed on your bare chest, something remarkable happens. Their tiny body, freshly introduced to the world, begins to absorb your warmth, steadying their own temperature. Their heartbeat even synchronizes with yours. The smell of your skin, the sound of your voice, and the gentle caress of your hands are the first sensory experiences your baby encounters.

How can you optimize this golden hour?

1. **Stay Present:** Engage in the moment fully. This isn't the time to snap endless photos or update your social media. It's a time to connect, undisturbed, with your newborn.

2. **Be Shirt-Ready:** Prepare to give your baby all the skin-to-skin contact they need. This might mean unbuttoning your shirt in advance to create a cozy space for them.

3. **Speak Softly:** Your voice is a reassuring melody to your newborn. Gently talk or sing to them. They've heard your voice before from inside the womb, and it's a familiar, comforting sound.

4. **Gentle Touch:** Tiny, delicate strokes and the gentle placement of your hand on their back provide security and warmth.

5. **Embrace the Emotion:** Allow yourself to feel. If tears come, let them. It's a monumental moment that can be as overwhelming as it is joyful.

6. **Photography:** If you wish to capture the moment, perhaps ask a relative or professional to take candid shots, allowing you to be fully immersed in the experience.

It's essential to remember that the golden hour might not always go as planned. Situations like medical concerns with the baby or the birthing parent might necessitate temporary separation. In such instances, hold on to patience and hope, and embrace your baby as soon as it's safe to do so.

In the ensuing days of new fatherhood, recall the sensations and emotions of this golden hour. It's more than a memory; it's the starting point of your lifelong bond with your child. Their warm, fragile body against your chest, their soft, irregular breaths, and the incomparable sensation of their presence will be a wellspring of strength and love in the adventures and challenges that lie ahead in your parenting journey.

Post-Birth Connection

The voyage doesn't conclude with birth. The post-birth moments are equally vital, often filled with raw emotions and unfiltered expressions of relief, joy, and sometimes anxiety. Being present, offering a steady arm to lean on, and continuing to advocate for your partner's needs is as important as ever.

From a Woman's Perspective: Actionable, Practical Steps to Take

Based on my experience with my husband, there's a bunch of stuff your partner might not be telling you she's hoping for—especially on the big day and the week after. I'm going to break it down for you real simple, so you can ace this whole support gig. Let's get to it!

Stay Calm, Don't Panic: During the intense moments of labor, she needs you to be her support and do or say whatever necessary to keep her calm. Even if it seems like a panic attack is looming, maintaining composure is essential. If you lose your composure, she may also lose hers.

- **Action Steps:** In the delivery room, focus on being the calming force. Practice keeping your cool, use humor appropriately, and show confidence. This positive energy, along with lots of words of encouragement, will help your partner feel more secure and supported.
- **Pro Tip:** If you're a faint risk at the sight of blood, please inform the staff beforehand. They'll get you a chair and position you away from your partner's bottom half.

Notice Non-Verbal Cues: In the throes of labor, your partner might not be able to communicate verbally. It's crucial to be attuned to her non-verbal cues, which can communicate discomfort, pain, or other needs.

- **Action Steps:** Be observant and attentive to subtle cues, such as discomfort or a need for rest. Proactively offer support, like adjusting pillows or providing water, without waiting for a verbal request. If you see beads of sweat trickling down her forehead, go ahead and wipe it with a damp cloth.

Understand the Birth Lingo: Understanding the medical terms used in the delivery room will help you grasp the situation better and provide her with reassurance that you're both prepared. She doesn't want you Googling things in the middle of labor—and you may not even have time to do so.

- **Action Steps:** Learn the basics of childbirth-related medical terminology. While you don't need to be an expert, having a general understanding will aid in communication with health care providers and enable you to support your partner more effectively.

Embrace these tips, and you'll not only ease the journey for your partner, but also strengthen the bond within your growing family. Trust in yourself, stay engaged, and get ready for one of the most rewarding experiences of your life. You've got this!

Key Takeaways

Stepping into fatherhood is a life-changing event that is as emotional as it is rewarding. In this chapter, we explored the essence of becoming a dad and how to navigate this new journey with grace and presence.

- **Tears Equal Strength:** Showing emotion at your child's birth is a profound display of love, not weakness.
- **Bond in the First Hour:** Use the golden hour after birth for skin-to-skin contact to establish a deep connection with your newborn.
- **Be Prepared and Present:** Arm yourself with practical and emotional tools to support your partner through labor.
- **Continuous Support:** Offer ongoing assistance to your partner after birth, through both action and empathy.

Navigating fatherhood from the first moments of birth is about expressing vulnerability, fostering early connections, actively participating in labor, and providing unwavering support. These actions lay a strong emotional foundation for the family and epitomize your evolving role as a father.

Chapter Seven
THE FIRST 48 HOURS: HOSPITAL PROCEDURES AND CARING FOR YOUR NEWBORN

"Embracing the chaos of the first moments means truly living in the beauty of fatherhood."

—*Jake Harrison*

Thiple first 48 hours after your little one's grand entrance into the world can feel like you've been handed the most precious puzzle, but without the instruction manual. It's all about adapting to new routines, coming to grips with hospital protocols, and decoding a bunch of different baby cries that sound confusingly similar.

Facing this initial phase might stir memories of simpler challenges, like mastering that complex coffee machine or conquering the final level of a tricky video game. The good news is that, with the comprehensive advice in this book, you're about to transform from rookie to pro in no time. Remember, countless incredible dads have been right where you are now. Who knows—in a few years, you might be dishing out tips that have others calling you the "newborn whisperer" at future gatherings.

The Hospital Stay: What to Expect and How to Keep Your Cool

If someone had told me earlier that a hospital could feel like a battleground, I'd have chuckled. But when the moment came, it felt like the frontline of the most exhilarating and nerve-wracking event of my life. For many of you, the experience might be the same. It's crucial to understand that the length of your hospital stay can vary depending on circumstances. With an uncomplicated vaginal birth, expect to remain for 24 to 48 hours. For C-sections, the stay extends to two to four days.

The Bustle and the Lingo

In the first 48 hours after delivery, the hospital transforms into a whirlwind of activity. Doctors, nurses, midwives—everyone seems to be on their toes, often communicating in medical jargon that sounds like they're planning a space mission. But it's just their way of ensuring that both your partner and your baby get the best care. As a new dad, you might not understand every term or acronym thrown around, but don't shy away from asking. There's no silly question here, especially when it's about the well-being of your family.

Visitors and "Me Time"

During the initial 48 hours after delivery, you're typically in the hospital, where guest policies often limit the number of visitors. It's important to carefully consider who makes it onto this exclusive guest list, if you choose to have one at all. Remember, you and your partner will be exhausted, and any visitors should be sources of support, not stress. It's perfectly okay to want time alone to recuperate and bond with your baby.

Tests and Checks

Newborns undergo a series of routine checks to ensure they're healthy. These might include hearing tests, heart screenings, and the like. It's easy to get anxious, but remember, these are standard procedures. The medical team is experienced in handling newborns. If you're curious about a particular test, get the lowdown from the pediatrician. They know what they are doing and are usually more than willing to share.

Overnight Stays and Sleep (or Lack of It)

Hospital stays after delivery can resemble a sleepover, but with a twist—minimal sleep. Between regular feedings, health checks, and your newborn's cries, uninterrupted sleep is a rare commodity. You'll find your slumber frequently interrupted as the staff diligently checks on Mom and Baby's vitals. Although challenging, it's essential to try and rest. Embrace those brief moments of respite, even if it's just a 20-minute power nap. They can be surprisingly rejuvenating.

Keeping Your Cool

No one's handing out medals for "The Most Chill Dad in the Maternity Ward," but maintaining a level head is still important. It's not just about being there physically, but also being present emotionally. There's a ton of emotion packed into these 48 hours—joy, anxiety, exhaustion, and euphoria. Take deep breaths, step out for a quick walk if you need to, and remember that it's okay to seek support.

These initial hours are a blend of incredible moments and a number of challenges. There's a steep learning curve, but you're not climbing alone. You have a partner, medical professionals, and a network of fellow dads. Embrace the experience.

Apgar Score, Hearing Tests, and Other Screenings: Monitoring Your Baby's Health

Remember the thrill of bringing home a new gadget? That impulse to pore over every spec, detail, and feature? Now, amplify that feeling tenfold. You've just welcomed a living, breathing baby into the world, but, unlike your latest tech toy, this little one doesn't come with a manual. Fortunately, the hospital has some initial screenings lined up for your newborn to ensure they're kicking off life on the right foot.

1. The Apgar Score: The First Test

Within the first few minutes of your baby's life, a nurse or doctor will assign an Apgar score. This is a quick assessment based on five factors: heart rate, breathing, muscle tone, reflexes, and skin color. Each factor scores between 0 and 2, with a maximum total score of 10.

I recall my competitive spirit rising when I heard about this. "You're saying my son can score on something already? Let's go for the 10!" But as it turns out, a perfect score isn't essential. Babies often score between 7 and 9, and that's perfectly fine. It's just a first-glance tool to check if any immediate medical assistance is needed.

2. Hearing Tests: Sound Check!

One of the primary screenings your baby will undergo is the hearing test. This is essential, as early detection of hearing problems can pave the way for interventions that help with speech and language development.

The test is simple and non-intrusive. The baby wears tiny earphones, and the doctors play sounds to see if the ears respond. I remember thinking it was like the baby's first concert, only a bit quieter.

3. Blood Screening: A Tiny Pinprick

Your newborn will also have a small blood sample taken, usually from their heel. This helps to detect various conditions, including thyroid disorders, sickle cell disease, and other metabolic disorders. The prick is quick, and while your baby might protest a bit, they'll soon settle down.

Keeping Things in Perspective

Hearing about these tests can be a tad overwhelming, but remember, they're all standard procedures that have your baby's best interests at heart. As a new dad, your job is to offer comfort. Holding your baby's hand or softly humming a tune can make all the difference during these tests.

Tech Tip: If you're digitally inclined, most hospitals now have portals where you can log in and check your baby's test results. This might be useful if you like to keep a digital health record for your family.

Lean On Your Dad Squad

If you ever feel anxious about these tests, reach out to fellow fathers. I guarantee that most dads have been through the same roller coaster of emotions. Sharing stories, especially ones sprinkled with a dash of humor, can ease those nerves. One of my friends joked that his baby's hearing test felt like introducing his son to his favorite rock band. These light-hearted moments and shared camaraderie can make the journey smoother.

These initial screenings are just a small part of the fantastic journey of fatherhood. They're designed to give your baby the best start possible. Embrace the tests, trust the process, and, most importantly, enjoy every moment with your newborn.

Jaundice and Other Concerns: Things to Watch Out for in the Early Days

Dave, a good friend of mine, called me in a slight panic when his newborn turned a peculiar shade of yellow. "Is my kid auditioning for 'The Simpsons?'" he quipped, trying to mask his concern with humor.

That was Dave's introduction to jaundice. While his joke was unique, the situation wasn't—many newborns experience this.

The Yellow Fellow: Understanding Jaundice

Jaundice is a common condition where a baby's skin and the whites of their eyes turn yellow. This yellowing happens due to a buildup of bilirubin, a substance produced when red blood cells break down. In most cases, the liver filters it out. But since newborns' livers are still getting up to speed, bilirubin can sometimes accumulate.

Most jaundice is harmless and resolves on its own. However, it's essential to monitor. In some cases, the baby may receive one to two days of phototherapy treatment if bilirubin levels get too high.

Other Newborn Quirks to Note

1. **Mottled Skin:** It's not uncommon for a baby's skin to appear blotchy or mottled, especially if they're cold. This patchy look is due to the baby's circulatory system's development. As long as the baby warms up and the mottling goes away, all is good.
2. **Sticky Eyes:** Sometimes, newborns can have sticky eyes due to blocked tear ducts. Gently cleaning the eyes with cooled boiled water usually does the trick. If it persists, a quick chat with your pediatrician will set your mind at ease.

3. **Funny Shaped Head:** Don't be alarmed if your baby's head looks slightly elongated or misshapen. The process of birth can mold a baby's head temporarily, giving it a cone-like appearance. This usually settles in a few days.

4. **Baby Acne:** Breakouts aren't just for teenagers. Some newborns might develop baby acne, which are tiny red or white bumps on their faces. These are typically harmless and clear up on their own.

It's okay to worry—every first-time dad does. But remember, babies, like the rest of us, have their quirks. Most of these initial concerns are usually just that—initial. They fade as quickly as they appear. However, always trust your gut. If something feels off or you're unsure, never hesitate to seek professional advice. In the end, you're doing an incredible job, and every hiccup is just part of the journey in mastering the new dad code.

Lanugo, Vernix, and Other Newborn Quirks: Embracing the Uniqueness

The big moment arrives and your newborn is finally handed to you, but instead of the rosy, pudgy baby you might've expected from countless movies, you're introduced to a baby covered in...stuff. I remember that moment, and trust me, I was very surprised. No, the baby didn't decide to have a mini-spa day inside the womb. What you're seeing are nature's little gifts—lanugo and vernix.

Lanugo: The soft, fine hair covering your newborn's body is lanugo. This hair kept them warm inside the womb before their fat layers developed. While it might seem strange, it's totally natural and typically sheds within a few weeks after birth.

Vernix: The white, creamy substance covering your little one is called vernix. Think of it as a built-in moisturizer, protecting the baby's skin from the surrounding amniotic fluid. Without it, they'd be as wrinkly as a prune when they emerged! It also provides a slick runway for birth.

Soft Spots (Fontanelles): You might notice a soft spot or two on your baby's head. It's not a design flaw! These gaps in their skull make it flexible for birth and allow room for their brain to grow. They'll close up over time.

Blue Feet and Hands: If your baby has bluish hands and feet, don't panic. It's called acrocyanosis. Newborns' circulatory systems are still figuring things out, and this is just a temporary effect.

A buddy of mine named Steve became a dad a few months before I did. He was genuinely concerned that his baby girl was turning into the abominable snowman because of the lanugo. We had a good laugh when he found out it was entirely normal. Just imagine that conversation: "Honey, do we have any werewolves in our ancestry?"

Before you jump to any wild conclusions, remember, each baby is unique, and these quirks are just temporary phases in their development. In this digital age, you might be tempted to Google every odd thing you observe. While being informed is fantastic, remember that not everything online is accurate or applicable to your baby. When in doubt, always consult your pediatrician.

Baby's First Hospital Bath: Tips for a Gentle and Enjoyable Experience

Steve and I were hanging out at our usual sports bar, with him proudly flashing photos of his newborn son. But amidst his stories of late-night feedings and diaper changes, he confided, "Man, that first bath in the hospital? I was more nervous than when I faced that bull-charge linebacker back in college!"

The first bath of your little one can indeed feel like you're handling a bar of wet soap: slippery, delicate, and you're always afraid of dropping it. But with the right knowledge and a dash of patience, it can become a wonderful bonding moment.

Bath Time Strategy

- Keep a sharp eye on the nurses during the first bath—they're the pros. Ask questions and join in if they offer.
- Make sure the bath water is warm—use your elbow to test.
- Try swaddle bathing to keep the baby warm and calm, exposing only the parts you're washing.
- Use just a bit of gentle, baby-safe wash if needed, not a full lather.
- Never let go. One hand should always be securing the baby.
- Gentle water flow is key—think a calming stream, not a shower hose.
- Stay relaxed to help the baby chill. You'll both get better with practice.
- After the bath, snuggle your baby up in a towel for some cuddle time.

Starting Breastfeeding: How Dads Can Help

Breastfeeding isn't just "open baby's mouth, insert nipple." It's tricky and can be really challenging. Mom can struggle to get Baby latched on right, and man, can it hurt! We're talking cracked skin, soreness, and even bleeding. Dads, your support is key, so it is important that you educate yourself about the process.

First things first, the early milk called colostrum is like the pre-game show—it doesn't last long, but it's packed with good stuff for the baby. A few days in, the real milk arrives—along with a bunch of common hurdles:

- **Tongue-tie:** When the baby's tongue is anchored too tight to the bottom of their mouth.
- **Clogged ducts:** Kind of like a traffic jam in Mom's milk supply routes.
- **Mastitis:** A painful, often red and swollen breast area.

Here's how you can help:

- **Ice packs:** Keep 'em ready for sore boobs.
- **Hydration station:** Moms need to drink up, like an athlete— about 16 cups a day.
- **Lactation cookies:** They're like performance snacks for milk- making. Plus, they taste good.
- **Lactation consultants:** They've got the know-how, so when they're giving tips, take notes.

When it's go-time for feeding, think of it as setting up the perfect play. Your job is to help Mom and Baby get comfy and get the positioning down. According to my wife, having me as her "lactation coach" and offering a second pair of hands was a game-changer.

Hello Belly Button: Keeping the Cord Stump Clean and Happy

I was at the coffee machine in the office when Greg, a colleague with that distinct look of recent sleep deprivation, approached me. "So," he started, glancing around, "you've been there. Tell me, how did you deal with that weird-looking thing on the baby's belly? Kinda freaking me out!"

Ah, yes, the mysterious world of the umbilical cord stump. It can seem alien to many new dads, but I promise it isn't sci-fi—just simple science.

The Lowdown on the Stump

When babies are in the womb, they're attached to their mother's placenta via the umbilical cord. This is their lifeline, channeling essential nutrients to them. Once they enter our world, we snip that cord, leaving behind a tiny stump. This stump dries up and falls off within a few weeks, and voilà—a new belly button!

Taking Care of the Cord Stump

1. **Dry and Clean Is the Way:** The main goal is to keep it dry. Sponge baths are the best strategy until the stump is gone. If it gets wet accidentally, a simple pat down with a clean cloth does the trick.

2. **Let It Breathe:** Giving the stump some air can help speed up the drying process. Opt for airy clothing, or sometimes even let your

baby go commando. But be ready for some unexpected "gifts" during those diaper-free times.

3. **Steer Clear of Friction:** Diapers and stumps don't mix. Avoid any rubbing by folding the diaper's front down and away, ensuring it doesn't cover the stump.

4. **No Touching:** It might look intriguing, but resist the urge to poke or prod. The stump will fall off on its own when it's good and ready.

If the stump appears a bit slimy or has a few blood spots, light spot cleaning is okay. But if there are signs like redness or an unpleasant odor, it's time to chat with your pediatrician.

The Great Fall

When the stump finally does fall off, it's a big moment. Greg sent me a photo with a caption, "It's gone! Party at my place?" While celebrating might be a stretch, it's undoubtedly a milestone.

Pro Digital Dad Tip: While you might be used to documenting every tiny life event on social media, maybe keep the stump's exit as an offline memory. Not every milestone needs a digital footprint.

Wrap Up

Tiny details, like looking after an umbilical stump, can make fatherhood seem both bizarre and daunting. But every challenge you overcome, no matter how small, equips you with more confidence. And remember, there's a legion of dads, including Greg and yours truly, who've seen it all, done it all, and have the milk-stained t-shirt to prove it. We're in this together, navigating the wild ride of fatherhood one belly button at a time.

Snip or Skip? The Circumcision Conundrum

I remember sitting in that pastel-colored room at the pediatrician's office with Mike, a long-time buddy of mine. His firstborn son was snoozing soundly on his lap, wrapped snugly in a blanket. With wide eyes, Mike whispered, "Man, they've asked about circumcision. What did you do?"

Circumcision—the surgical removal of the foreskin covering the tip of the penis—is a decision many new dads grapple with. It's personal, and often influenced by cultural, religious, or medical factors. Let's unpack the choice without getting too knotted up.

Understanding Circumcision

Circumcision has been around for thousands of years, having its roots in religious rituals, especially in Jewish and Islamic communities. But beyond religious reasons, some opt for circumcision due to potential health benefits, while others might be influenced by cultural or societal factors.

The Pros and Cons

Benefits:

1. **Hygiene:** It's believed that circumcision can make it easier to clean the penis.
2. **Health Benefits:** Some studies suggest it reduces the risk of urinary tract infections, penile cancer, and the transmission of certain sexually transmitted infections.

Drawbacks:

1. **Risk of Complications:** As with any surgical procedure, there's the potential for complications, such as bleeding or infection.
2. **Pain:** Babies might experience pain, and there's the challenge of ensuring the area heals without complications.

The Decision Dilemma

This decision can feel like a weighty one. I chose not to circumcise my son based on personal beliefs, but every family's decision will be unique. It's essential to consult with your pediatrician, discuss with your partner, and perhaps even seek input from family or community members. Mike decided to hold off and give it more thought, leaning into that invaluable dad network for advice and shared experiences.

A Digital Dad's Approach: If you're the type who likes to research, there are tons of online resources available. Though it's crucial to lean on reputable websites and medical journals, remember to maintain a balanced perspective. Forums can be a rabbit hole of opinions. While they provide a window into real-life experiences, they might not always present the full picture.

Handling Emotions

It's natural to feel a myriad of emotions around the decision, including confusion, pressure, and even guilt. The key is to remember you're making the best choice for your family based on the information you have and the values you hold dear. When in doubt, seeking support, whether from fellow dads or professionals, can make the journey smoother.

No matter what you end up deciding, this is just one of many choices you'll make as a father. As I told Mike, being a dad isn't about making perfect decisions; it's about doing what you believe is best for your child, given the circumstances and information at hand. As you grow into your role, trust your instincts. They'll rarely steer you wrong.

Poop Colors 101: Decoding the Rainbow of Baby Poo

If you told me a few years ago that I'd be examining various shades of poo with the same attention as a detective looking for clues at a crime scene, I'd have chuckled. Yet, here we are, diving deep into the palette of baby poop colors! It's an odd topic, I know, but it's crucial to decode the mystery behind those diapers and understand what's normal and what isn't.

1. Black and Tar-Like: The Debut Poo

The first poop your newborn produces will be black and sticky, resembling tar. It's called meconium, and it's made up of everything your baby ingested while in the womb, from amniotic fluid to mucus. It's perfectly normal, albeit a bit tricky to clean up. **Pro Tip:** Stock up on baby wipes!

2. Transitioning to Greenish-Brown

After the initial black phase, you'll notice a transition to a greenish-brown hue. This is a sign that your baby's digestive system is starting its engines. As a fellow dad once said to me, "Think of it as the booting up phase for their tiny tummies."

3. Mustard Yellow: The Golden Standard

Breastfed babies tend to produce a light mustard-yellow poop with a soft, almost paste-like consistency. It might have tiny white seeds in it. Bottle-fed babies might have a slightly firmer, tan-colored poop. Both are normal.

4. Green Poop

This can be a fun topic among dads. One friend of mine swears his baby's green poo looked like a superhero's signature color. Green can be common in babies, and can indicate they're getting more low-calorie, watery milk than the richer milk that comes later in the feed. If you see this regularly, consult with your pediatrician or lactation expert.

5. Spotting the Red Flags

Bright red streaks can indicate blood. This might be a minor issue, like a small anal tear, but it's always wise to consult your pediatrician. Also, white or clay-colored poop can suggest a liver problem and requires immediate attention.

The Digital Diaper Log

If you have a knack for organizing data and a good sense of humor, consider starting a digital log or a detailed spreadsheet to track your baby's diaper changes. This log should include frequency, colors, and textures, noting anything unusual that stands out. Luckily, there are also a ton of free apps out there that can help you track the poo with ease! While it might seem like an odd collection of data, it actually serves two very practical purposes.

Firstly, it's an invaluable record to discuss with your pediatrician to ensure your baby's digestive system is working as it should. Health care professionals often request this information, especially in the early days in the hospital, and recommend continuing it at home.

Tracking these details helps to quickly identify what's normal and what might warrant a closer look.

Secondly, it will be a treasure trove of stories for the future. Imagine telling your child, "I have documented every hue of your first year's poos." It's a unique way to bond and remember these early days.

In the first few weeks, what's normal can vary widely. Newborns typically have several wet diapers a day, and at least three bowel movements, though some may have up to five or more. The first stools, called meconium, are thick and dark, but they change to yellowish-brown or green as babies start feeding. Keep an eye on consistency, frequency, and color changes—your pediatrician can provide a chart for reference. Digital tracking makes it easy to spot trends and anomalies over time, ensuring that your little one is on the right track.

From a Woman's Perspective: Actionable, Practical Steps to Take

Reflecting on our initial days with our newborn, I realize there were moments where my husband's understanding and teamwork could have eased our journey into parenthood. To all the new dads out there, learn from our experience to better navigate the early days with your baby. Here's what I wish my husband had known, and what you can do:

Daily Learning Exchange: Those first 48 hours are a steep learning curve! There's so much to learn and react to, and so many decisions to make. It gets overwhelming really fast. Share new things you've learned or mistakes that you've made. You might even brainstorm ideas or hacks to improve your quality of life!

- **Action Steps:** Make time each day to share what you've learned about your baby, no matter how small it might seem. This practice can strengthen your role as co-parents and enhance your connection with your child.

Managing the New Chaos: The chaos of bringing your newborn home is a new challenge. Your once orderly home quickly turns into a landscape of baby gear, laundry, and constant clutter. Your partner is hoping for more patience and humor from you in handling these changes.

- **Action Steps:** Embrace the disorder and unpredictability that comes with a newborn. When overwhelmed, take a moment to breathe and share a laugh together. Remember, it's about adapting and growing together, not about being perfect.

Fostering Forgiveness: During those first stressful days, you may need to be more forgiving and understanding, especially when exhaustion affects her moods and interactions.

- **Action Steps:** If tensions arise, try to step back and approach the situation with forgiveness. Recognize the stress both of you are under and prioritize compassion and empathy.

Coping with Sleep Deprivation: Sleep deprivation is a real challenge for mothers. Your wife will need more support from you in finding ways for both of you to rest and recharge.

- **Action Steps:** Create a schedule that allows both of you to take breaks for rest or relaxation. Even a short nap or a peaceful shower can make a significant difference in your ability to care for your newborn and each other.

Focus on practical learning, patience, and support. These early days with your newborn may be challenging, but by sharing knowledge, forgiving each other's mistakes, and ensuring rest, you'll navigate this new phase more effectively.

Key Takeaways

In the first two days with your new baby, you'll learn hospital rules and how to be there for your baby. You will also notice normal things like skin color changes and different kinds of baby poop. Here's a recap!

- **Understanding Hospital Routines:** The first step is learning hospital protocols and being proactive in newborn care during the many health checks and screenings.
- **Staying Emotionally Present:** New fathers should be emotionally available, manage visitors to ensure family bonding and rest, and offer comfort during their newborn's first vaccinations and tests.
- **Understanding Jaundice:** Jaundice in newborns is common and typically harmless, characterized by a yellowing of the skin and eyes due to the accumulation of bilirubin.
- **Recognizing Newborn Norms:** Many quirks in newborns, such as mottled skin, sticky eyes, funny-shaped heads, and baby acne, are normal and often resolve on their own. Parents should observe these conditions, but not panic, consulting a pediatrician if concerns persist.
- **Support in Breastfeeding Is Crucial:** Be ready with ice packs, hydration, and hands-on help for comfort and latch.
- **Baby Poop Variation:** The newborn poop color spectrum includes black meconium at birth, transitioning to greenish-

brown and then mustard yellow, especially in breastfed babies, with changes indicating the baby's digestive health.

- **Importance of Tracking:** Documenting your baby's poop color and texture is crucial for identifying normal digestive function and alerting you to potential health issues, which can be vital for pediatrician assessments. Download a baby app for you and your partner to get in sync!

Those first days are busy, but you've got this! Keep an eye on your baby's health signs, stay connected, and jot down what you notice. This is the beginning of a long and exciting road!

Chapter Eight

NURTURING YOUR RELATIONSHIP: LOVE, LAUGHTER, AND TEAMWORK

"Couples who laugh together, last together."

— *Dr. John Gottman*

Entering the world of fatherhood is exhilarating, but as every veteran dad will tell you, the heart of this journey is the relationship you share with your partner. It's the foundation upon which your new family is built. Strengthening that bond during the transition to parenthood is crucial. Both excitement and tension can brew during this time, but with a focus on love, a good dose of humor, and an unwavering sense of teamwork, the two of you can thrive together.

Many first-time fathers focus intently on their newborns, and unintentionally sideline their partners. But it's essential to remember that both of you are entering this new territory together. Think of it as being on a team where every player has a unique role, and every role is vital to the team's success.

This new phase of life will challenge your relationship in ways you might not have anticipated. Sleepless nights, mood swings, and the pressures of parenting can create friction. But they can also offer moments of profound connection, shared joy, and collective pride.

By putting in the effort to nurture your relationship during these times, you're not just investing in your partnership, but also ensuring a stable, loving environment for your child. Consider the strategies and insights shared in this book as tools in your relationship toolkit. Use them wisely, and remember that every challenge faced together makes the bond between you even stronger.

The Love Language of Parenthood: Keeping the Spark Alive

The dynamic between you and your partner is going to shift big time, especially in the first few months after childbirth. This isn't necessarily a bad thing, but it does require some effort to keep that initial passion and connection alive as you are adjusting to your new roles as mom and dad.

Recall the times when date nights were spontaneous—when you'd enjoy a late movie or a leisurely dinner. While it may feel like those carefree days are a thing of the past, they're simply transforming. As you step into the role of a father, the ways you express love and maintain connection with your partner will naturally adapt and grow. Embrace this change as part of your journey, finding new and creative ways to nurture your relationship amidst your evolving responsibilities.

Parenthood can bring you closer than ever before. It's all about finding new ways to connect. This can be as simple as a wink across the room while your partner is feeding the baby or leaving a sweet note for her to find when she wakes up for the early morning feed.

Gary Chapman's famed concept of the "Five Love Languages" resonates here. If you're not familiar, Chapman suggests that people express and interpret love in five primary ways: words of affirmation, acts of service, giving/receiving gifts, quality time, and physical touch. Apply this to your current situation. Perhaps your partner's love language was quality time, and now, with a baby, that time seems scarce. The key is to be more intentional. Even 10 minutes of focused conversation after the baby goes to sleep can make a world of difference.

Sometimes, it's the unrequested actions that speak volumes. Jumping in to handle baby care tasks can be a powerful way to show your partner she is valued. Instead of waiting to be told what's needed, be observant and take initiative. This proactive approach can be a significant relief for a new mom, as it spares her from the extra work of directing and explaining. Simple acts, like changing a diaper or soothing the baby without being prompted, are small but meaningful ways to support each other during this new chapter.

It's also crucial to remember that this phase, like all things, is temporary. Your relationship with your partner, on the other hand, is forever. The small gestures you make now will set the foundation for a deeper, more profound connection as you both navigate the beautiful journey of parenthood.

A friend of mine once joked that, after having kids, he and his wife became "high-efficiency communicators." Long-winded discussions were replaced by short, concise sentences between diaper changes and baby feeds. But they made it work, injecting humor into their interactions, laughing off the small stuff, and making every second of "us" time count.

Parenthood will challenge and change your relationship, but with love, laughter, and a sense of teamwork, you can keep the spark alive and fan it into an ever bigger flame.

Emotional Support: Understanding and Meeting Each Other's Needs

In my early days of fatherhood, I remember sitting in our living room, exhausted after another sleepless night, staring at my equally fatigued partner. Both of us were silently thinking, "When will this get easier?" It was in moments like these that I realized that while diapers and baby formula could be stocked up, emotional resilience was a different ball game.

Both of you are undergoing profound changes. While your partner deals with hormonal shifts, physical recovery, and the mental load of motherhood, you are grappling with the weight of newfound responsibilities and expectations. Fortunately, you're both in this together.

Acknowledge Each Other's Emotions

Understanding and valuing each other's emotions is key in nurturing your relationship during this time. Think of your partnership like an emotional bank account, where positive interactions are deposits and negative ones are withdrawals.

Your goal is to maintain a positive balance. Simple gestures like asking "How was your day?" or affirming "You're doing a great job" can contribute significantly to this. It's about recognizing and validating each other's feelings, whether through a supportive word, a shared laugh, or simply being present in a challenging moment. Every action that shows understanding and empathy is a deposit into this account, strengthening your bond and mutual support.

Active Listening Is Important

Active listening isn't just nodding your head while mentally preparing your grocery list. It's genuinely focusing on what your partner is saying without interrupting or immediately offering solutions. Often, they don't need you to "fix" things, they just want to be heard.

It's Okay to Seek Help

Sometimes, emotions can be overwhelming, and that's okay. Whether it's talking to a trusted friend, joining a new dads' group online, or seeking professional counseling, getting an external perspective can provide clarity.

Respect Each Other's Me Time

Remember those days when you'd lounge on the couch, binge-watching your favorite series? Parenthood might have changed the frequency of those days, but the need for personal space remains. Encourage your partner to take a break, and do the same for yourself. Whether it's a quick walk, a hobby, or just a power nap, it can recharge you both emotionally.

Understanding and meeting each other's emotional needs isn't complicated. By prioritizing emotional support, you not only strengthen your relationship, but also create a nurturing environment for your little one. And in those testing moments, always remember that better days filled with laughter and love await.

Navigating the New Terrain of Parenthood: A Team Effort

Once parenthood begins, a new level of exhaustion sets in—one that calls for unprecedented teamwork. Here's how to understand your new "normal" and keep the partnership thriving while juggling the joys and challenges of a new baby.

Embrace the Shifts

Managing the nighttime needs of a newborn requires a tactical approach. Consider assigning night duties to one parent, perhaps alternating based on each other's natural rhythms and work commitments. This method promotes better sleep for at least one partner, helps establish a predictable routine, and can reduce overall stress. Remember, it's less about a strict division and more about fluid teamwork that plays to each parent's strengths.

Divide Responsibly, Conquer Compassionately

While breastfeeding may be a one-parent job, there's a wide array of tasks awaiting the other. From diaper changes to lullabies, share the responsibilities. Use technology to your advantage—a shared digital calendar can be invaluable for tracking appointments, milestones, and tasks, ensuring both partners are informed and involved.

The Power of Delegation and Shared Knowledge

Don't be afraid to ask for help. When a neighbor offers to assist with errands or a family member offers to babysit, say yes. Meanwhile, both partners should stay informed about the baby's development and care requirements. Sharing knowledge can be as critical as sharing tasks—it shows commitment and keeps both parents engaged in the process.

Preserve Your Bond

In the whirlwind of new parenthood, it's vital to keep the connection between the two of you strong. Dedicate time for each other—be it a simple walk, a shared hobby, or a date night. It's not only about maintaining romance, but also about nurturing the partnership that forms the foundation of your growing family.

Effective Communication: Listening, Understanding, and Supporting Each Other

I still recall the night my partner, deep into her third trimester, burst into tears after a simple comment I made about her food choice. "You think I'm overeating," she sobbed.

Let me tell you, folks, it wasn't about the food. It was deeper—a combination of fears, hormones, and a need for reassurance. So, how do you bridge the gap when it feels like you're talking across an ever-widening canyon?

Words Are Only Part of the Story

Research has found that 70-93% of communication is non-verbal (body language, tone of voice, etc.). So, when she's saying everything's "fine" but looks like she's plotting revenge against the universe, trust the vibes. Observe, be intuitive, and ask gentle, open-ended questions.

The Power of "I" Statements

Starting a conversation with "You always" or "You never" is a direct ticket to Defensive land. Instead, try the "I feel...when..." approach. Instead of pointing fingers, express your emotions and perceptions. For instance, "I feel overwhelmed when we don't share household responsibilities" sounds way better than "You never help around the house."

The Digital Time-Out

In our hyper-connected era, distractions are everywhere. But when it comes to heart-to-heart conversations, it's a good idea to stash the gadgets. No checking football scores or work emails—give each other your undivided attention. Your relationship deserves that premium, ad-free experience.

Regular Relationship Check-Ins

You service your car, so why not your relationship? Set aside regular times to talk about how things are going. It can be over a home-cooked meal or during a quiet drive. The idea is to create a safe space where both of you can share freely, without judgment.

Finding Humor and Comfort

During the early stages of parenting, finding humor in everyday situations can be a wonderful way to ease stress. Sharing funny memes and videos about the adventures and misadventures of new parenthood helped my partner and me. These shared laughs brought us comfort, reminding us that we weren't alone in this crazy journey. We were part of a community facing similar joys, challenges and making many mistakes along the way. It was through laughter that we often found reassurance and a sense of normalcy in our new roles as parents.

Seek Outside Help If Needed

If communication challenges become a regular occurrence in your relationship, it might be time to consider couples therapy. Opting for therapy is not a sign of failure, but a proactive approach to enhancing your relationship with effective tools and strategies. It's important to break down the stigma surrounding counseling or therapy. It's nothing to be embarrassed about. Seeking professional help can be a transformative and empowering step, and might just save your sanity.

As you journey through the transformative experience of parenthood, keep in mind that open, genuine dialogue is the foundation of any strong relationship. While achieving perfection isn't necessary, every effort to improve communication is a step toward a more harmonious partnership.

Acts of Kindness: Small Gestures with a Big Impact

One evening, a friend of mine named Rob found himself in an interesting situation. He came home from work to discover that his wife had accidentally ordered a ridiculously large quantity of bananas from an online grocery store. Instead of sighing or laughing it off, Rob turned this into an evening activity. They made banana bread, banana smoothies, and even played a game of "Who can come up with the craziest banana recipe?" His act of turning a potential frustration into a fun, shared memory showcased an overlooked art in relationships: The language of small acts.

Mastering the Micro-Moment

Sometimes, it's the little things that speak volumes. Leaving a handwritten note by her bedside or simply filling up her water bottle might seem insignificant, but they're quiet whispers that say, "I'm here for you."

Task-Tackling Together

Turning chores into a joint activity can make them feel less mundane. Folding laundry? Turn it into a sock-matching race. Cooking dinner? How about a mini cook-off challenge? Infusing teamwork and humor into daily tasks can amplify your connection.

Acknowledging the Changes

Pregnancy brings about myriad physical and emotional changes. A simple, "You're doing amazing," or an unsolicited foot massage can be the balm for her tired soul.

Mind the Energy Gap

Realize that your partner might become drained faster than usual. Offer to handle some of her daily tasks, or, better yet, surprise her by doing them before she mentions it. Remember the banana incident with Rob? Think about how you can turn challenges into moments of connection.

Creating Shared Rituals

Be it a five-minute evening dance in the living room or a weekly game night, shared rituals can be the glue that keeps you close in these transformative months.

Expressing Gratitude

Amidst all the preparations and adjustments, it's easy to forget the power of a genuine "thank you." Expressing gratitude, even for the tiniest gestures, fosters a culture of appreciation.

Next time you're faced with a surplus of bananas or any unexpected twist, remember Rob's example. Use it as an opportunity to grow, bond, and find joy in the micro-moments. The journey might be full of unpredictable turns, but with acts of kindness, it's bound to be a memorable one.

Planning for the Future: Discussing Parenting Styles and Shared Goals

When my friends Mark and Linda were expecting their first child, they often disagreed about how to raise them. Mark had been raised in a strict household, and thought rules and discipline were key. Linda was from a more relaxed home and preferred a softer approach. At first, this caused some tension between them.

But as they talked more about it, they started to see the benefits in each other's methods. Mark realized Linda's flexible style could help their child be more creative and independent. Meanwhile, Linda saw that Mark's structured approach could give their child a sense of stability.

They decided to mix their styles. They agreed on clear rules for their child, but also wanted to be open to discussion and adaptability. This mix of structure and flexibility seemed like a good balance for them.

This story shows how important it is for parents to talk and find a middle ground that works for them both. Here are some steps to help you and your partner develop a shared approach to parenting:

Start With Self-Reflection

Before any discussion, both of you should spend some time separately considering your childhoods. What did you appreciate about how you were raised? What would you change? Mark realized that while he appreciated the discipline he grew up with, he didn't want his child to feel the same pressure he often felt.

Schedule Parenting Powwows

Setting aside regular times to discuss your thoughts can help keep things structured. For our digital dads out there, consider setting up a shared online document where both of you can jot down ideas as they come. This offers a dynamic way to keep the conversation going, even amidst busy schedules.

Use Humor as a Mediator

There was a time when Linda jokingly said their kid would only eat organic, farm-to-table baby food, and Mark countered with the idea of introducing the baby to fast food. It was all in jest, but humor has a way of diffusing tension and making tough conversations easier.

Understand, Don't Assume

Conflicts often arise from misunderstandings. Instead of presuming you know why your partner thinks a certain way, ask them. When Mark probed deeper into Linda's laid-back approach, he discovered it wasn't about being lax, but about fostering independence.

Flexibility Is Key

Even with all the planning in the world, unexpected challenges will arise. Being adaptable is crucial. Mark and Linda had to find a middle ground between their parenting styles. Their blend was unique to them and worked great.

Envision Shared Dreams

In addition to parenting styles, it's essential to discuss shared goals for your family. Do you dream of annual family vacations? Do you wish to instill a love for music or sports in your child? Aligning on these broader visions can guide smaller, day-to-day decisions.

By the time their little one arrived, Mark and Linda had laid down a solid foundation—a unique parenting style tailor-made for their family. Sure, they had their disagreements, but their commitment to understanding and adapting for the sake of their child made all the difference.

As you embark on this journey, remember that it's less about right and wrong and more about what works for your family. Through understanding, humor, and a shared vision, you and your partner can craft a parenting blueprint that's just right for your new family.

From a Woman's Perspective: Actionable, Practical Steps to Take

Navigating through this new chapter of parenthood, I stumbled, learned, and felt so many things that I wish my own husband had a clearer insight into. Here are a few insights I hope resonate with you:

Emotions Aren't a Straight Path: There'll be days when your partner might seem like a storm of feelings, and it might be best to stay clear of her when she's on the warpath. Remember, sometimes it's not *really* about you. These hormonal shifts have a way of making even the small things feel monumental.

- **Action Step #1:** Offer patience and understanding when her emotions fluctuate unpredictably. Give her some space and time to reflect and calm down.
- **Action Step #2:** Provide a pleasant, happy distraction, like a backrub or her favorite snack.

The Changing Body Can Be a Maze: Every new change in her body can sometimes feel foreign and overwhelming. The day that she finds that she can no longer fit her "regular underwear" or favorite pants can be a bittersweet moment. It's the realization that her body will never be the same again. Finding clothes that fit and look good can be quite challenging, especially when her body keeps changing.

- **Action Steps:** Regularly compliment her strength and beauty to uplift her through bodily changes. She wants to know that you're still attracted to her. Positive words go a long way to boost her self-confidence and help her keep a positive body image.

Exhaustion Isn't an Understatement: Growing a baby requires energy on levels I never imagined. It was a new feeling for me to be so lethargic and drained all the time. So when she retreats for a nap or wants an early night, it's her body and baby asking for a moment. Trust me, it's not just sleep. It's rejuvenation.

- **Action Steps:** Encourage and enable rest, recognizing it as essential for her and the baby's well-being. Take charge of any household or baby-related tasks that you are able to do. You want her to focus on two things: your newborn and herself.

Postpartum Adjustments: After the baby's arrival, your world and responsibilities shift dramatically. Your partner has just gone through one of the most painful days of her life. She has a long road of recovery ahead of her, physically, mentally, and emotionally. Her body needs time to heal, but on top of that, she has to say goodbye to her old self and accept her new self. She needs your support more now than ever.

- **Action Steps:** Be attentive to signs of postpartum stress or anxiety in both you and your partner. Offer a listening ear, share your own feelings, and work together to find ways to support each other as new parents. Remember, open communication and shared understanding are key to navigating this new chapter in your lives and relationship.

Key Takeaways

Maintaining a strong, supportive relationship after the baby is born is essential. Here's a quick recap:

- **Emotional Support:** Be understanding and patient as both of you navigate the new emotional landscape of parenthood. Offer comfort and empathy during this adjustment period.

- **Affirmation and Appreciation:** Regularly acknowledge and appreciate the efforts and changes your partner is going through as a new mother. Positive reinforcement can have a profound impact.

- **Encourage Rest and Recovery:** Recognize the importance of rest and recovery after childbirth. Help create a relaxing environment for your partner to recuperate.

- **Alleviate New Parent Anxieties:** Offer support and reassurance to help ease the common fears and anxieties associated with new parenthood.

- **Maintain Connection and Intimacy:** Proactively work to maintain emotional intimacy and connection with your partner. Keep the essence of your relationship alive amidst the new responsibilities.

By embracing these key aspects, you'll help strengthen your relationship during the transition into parenthood, ensuring a loving and supportive environment for your growing family.

Conclusion
BECOMING THE ULTIMATE NEW DAD

Fatherhood is more than just a title—it's an evolution, a transformative journey that reshapes the very core of a man. As you've navigated the pages of The New Dad Code, you've journeyed through the intricacies of becoming the best version of a dad—one that's both strong and sensitive, confident and humble, ready to lead and eager to learn. Whether you're embarking on this path for the first time or revisiting these lessons to refine your fatherhood skills, remember that every father's story is unique, yet also universally significant.

From the captivating first trimester, where the journey began with those life-altering words "We're pregnant," to the invigorating excitement of the second trimester and the anticipation of the third, you've discovered the transformative nature of fatherhood. You've learned about supporting and celebrating Mom, understanding your emotions, prepping for Baby, and ensuring the safety and comfort of your family. Every chapter offered tools, tips, and tidbits, not to mention the invaluable "Woman's Perspective" sections that provided insight into my partner's experience and advice.

While each chapter delved into unique phases of the pregnancy journey, the overarching theme of the book has always been about connection—connection with your partner, connection with your soon-to-be or newborn child, and connection with yourself. Navigating the social aspects of pregnancy, understanding the importance of mental health, and stepping up during the big day are all part of this narrative of connection.

Embrace every moment with an open heart, a listening ear, and proactive hands. Celebrate the joys, face challenges with courage, and always prioritize the well-being of Mom and Baby. While you're sure to face unexpected hurdles and moments of self-doubt, know that you're equipped with the knowledge, tools, and heart to rise to any occasion. The love you have for your family is the most potent tool you possess.

Take these lessons, insights, and tools, and use them as your compass. As you embark on this new chapter of life, remember to lean on your newfound knowledge, and on each other. Becoming a father isn't a solo expedition, it's a shared adventure—one where teamwork, love, and understanding are essential.

If The New Dad Code has resonated with you—if it has made you laugh, made you think, or better prepared you for the joys of fatherhood—consider sharing your journey with others. Every dad out there is looking for guidance, and your insights and experiences could be the help they need. Please consider leaving a review on Amazon. Every word can make a world of difference for another dad out there.

Finally, take a moment to acknowledge the love, laughter, and learning that's come your way. As you look forward to the joys and challenges of fatherhood, remember that you are not alone. You have a community, a partner, and now, a guide. The New Dad Code isn't just a book; it's a pledge to being present, loving, and supportive.

Step boldly into the world of fatherhood. Embrace the adventure. Cherish every moment. Welcome to the wonderful world of being a dad.

Get Your <u>Free</u> Bonuses Now!

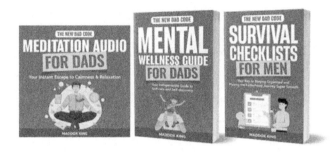

BONUS # 1: Survival Checklists for Dads
Your Key to Staying Organized and Making the Pregnancy Journey Super Smooth!

BONUS # 2: Mental Wellness Guide for Dads
Your Indispensable Guide to Self-care and Self-discovery, Ensuring a Journey Towards a Happier and More Fulfilled You!

BONUS # 3: Meditation Audio for Dads
Your Instant Escape to Calmness, Relaxation, and Well-deserved Quality "Me Time."

Scan with your phone's camera **OR** go to: https://bit.ly/41Q7CJU

Printed in Great Britain
by Amazon

46317254R00106